This book has been designed to support students studying GCSE Home Economics: Child Development or GNVQ Health and Social Care. It may be used as an aid to teaching and learning throughout the course and also as a revision guide prior to the terminal examination. The subject matter is presented in a straightforward, spacious manner with clear concise diagrams throughout, in order to support a variety of learning styles.

This guide has been checked against the exam board specifications for examination in 2007 onward. Where necessary the content has been revised or supplemented to ensure the guide remains accurate and relevant.

The author would like to convey her thanks to Andrea Brewis (Registered Midwife) for her valuable contributions throughout; to The Princess Alexandra Hospital, NHS Trust, Harlow; and special thanks to Jessica, James, Lucy, Edward, Ellena, William, Georgia and Thomas.

D0314121

AUTHOR: **Judi Sunderland - Examiner for GCSE Child Development, Lecturer in Child Development for SFE and Advanced Skills Teacher**

EDITORS: **Jo Hill & Rebecca Skinner**

MEDICAL CONSULTANT: **Dr G. J. Parsons M.B.ch.B, D.R.C.O.G.**

The publishers would like to thank:
J. Sainsbury's, Shorehead, Huddersfield - Making Life Taste Better; Boots The Chemists, Huddersfield; Shaw & Hallas Ltd, Huddersfield; The Huddersfield Royal Infirmary; Looby Loo's, Holmfirth; Camphill Rudolf Steiner Schools, Aberdeen

They also send a special thank you to Grace, James, Esther, Sam, Charlie, Louis, Tom, Hayley, Issy and Andrew.

● CONTENTS

CONTENTS

What is a Family?

A family is the BASIC UNIT OF SOCIETY. It plays a vital role in the growth and development of children. Traditionally, a family is a group of people who live together and are related by birth (blood), adoption or marriage. Nowadays many couples 'CO-HABIT', i.e. they live together as a family but are not married. Family structures can change.

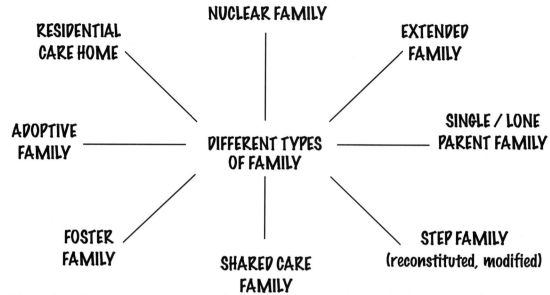

NB Some countries have very different family structures e.g. the 'kibbutz' community in Israel.

Nuclear, Extended and Step Families

	ADVANTAGES	DISADVANTAGES
NUCLEAR FAMILY This consists of parents and children who live together in a home separate from the rest of the family (extended family).	• There is no interference from their extended family on a daily basis. • They can choose when to visit the extended family.	• Children and grandparents may not have close relationships if separated by long distances. • Close family relationships will require special effort and hard work. • Non-family members will have to be paid for childcare. • Emergency childcare may not be available.
EXTENDED FAMILY Similar to nuclear family though 'extended' (made bigger) by the addition of grandparents, aunts, uncles and cousins. They all live in the same house, or close to each other, so they can easily meet on a regular basis.	• There are people to offer advice and give practical help e.g. look after children. • There may be financial advantages. • Close family bonds can be formed. • Children may have cousins to play with.	• There may be a lack of privacy. • There may be a lack of independence and unwanted advice may be offered. • There may be different approaches to child rearing, leading to friction.
STEP FAMILY This is a blending of families. It is formed when a couple, at least one of whom has a child (or children), marry or co-habit. This new relationship may result in more children (step-brothers or step-sisters). 18 million people are part of a step family.	• The family may have a better quality of life. • There may be more income. • The children have both male and female role models.	• Children may not bond with the step-parent and may resent them. • Sibling rivalry is common, especially amongst children of similar ages. • Children may have limited access to their biological parent.

Single Parent and Shared Care Families

SINGLE PARENT FAMILY

The vast majority of single / lone parents are mothers who bring up children on their own. More than 25% of children are brought up in this situation. Contrary to popular belief only 3% of single parents are under the age of 20.

Death of one parent
(widow/widower)

Adoption by a
single person

Birth to a single woman
a woman's personal choice;
father unknown; use of sperm bank;
as a result of rape

REASONS FOR SINGLE PARENT FAMILIES

Absence of one parent
e.g. due to work (army posting abroad),
illness or imprisonment

Divorce or
separation of parents

Surrogacy
arrangement

ADVANTAGES	DISADVANTAGES
• Parent can make decisions independently. • Child may be happier if removed from a stressful situation created by two parents.	• Child lacks role model of absent parent. • Parent has no one to discuss problems with. • Hard work for parent physically, financially and emotionally.

SHARED CARE FAMILY

The divorce or separation of parents may mean that children live in two households, spending time with both parents. Their everyday care and upbringing remains the equal responsibility of both parents. Decisions that affect them are made jointly

Other Types of Families

ADOPTIVE FAMILY

Adoption provides a permanent home for a child whose parents are unable to do so. Adoptive parents come from a wide variety of backgrounds and must undergo extensive and rigorous checks by Social Services to ensure their suitability. This also applies if a child is adopted abroad. When an adoption is finalised in court the adoptive parents assume all the rights and responsibilities of the birth parents. The child usually takes the new family name.

RESIDENTIAL CARE HOME

Small groups of children are looked after by carers in a family-type structure. Care homes are run by Social Services and are designed to provide only short-term care.

FOSTER FAMILY

There are many different reasons why children cannot be looked after by their natural parents and so are placed in either long- or short-term foster care. Foster parents may be married, single or co-habiting with people of either sex, with or without their own children. They must be thoroughly checked to ensure they are suitable carers by Social Services who will then provide them with training. When children are put into their care they will be paid by the Local Authority and supported by Social Services who will have the legal responsibility for them. Foster children are normally encouraged to maintain contact with their birth families with the aim that they can be reunited. If this is not possible then they may be placed for adoption.

The Changing Structure of Families

Families are changing all the time as circumstances alter. Some reasons include:

- Couples expect a certain lifestyle and have different attitudes to those of their parents.
- New laws have made it easier for couples to DIVORCE.
- People marry and have children at a later age.
- The state provides money to support single-parent families.
- Social and moral attitudes have changed; co-habitation, pregnancy outside marriage, and single parents are now acceptable.
- Improved contraception allows people to choose to have fewer children and to plan when they'll be born.

Family Roles

Roles within families differ and are becoming more complex and difficult to define especially after divorce, re-marriage or when people co-habit.

SEXUAL ROLES are determined by NATURE (genes) or NURTURE (the environment in which a child is raised). It is a debatable point which of the two has the greatest influence but both are important.

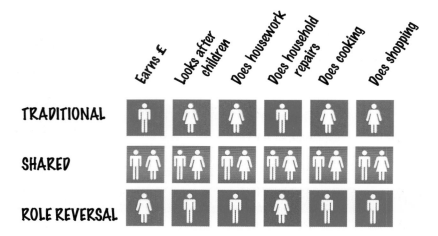

	Earns £	Looks after children	Does housework	Does household repairs	Does cooking	Does shopping
TRADITIONAL	man	woman	woman	man	woman	woman
SHARED	man+woman	man+woman	man+woman	man+woman	man+woman	man+woman
ROLE REVERSAL	woman	man	man	woman	man	man

Stereotyping

SEXUAL STEREOTYPING is a result of what children see in society and their own homes, and the way in which they are brought up (e.g. most builders are men, most shop assistants are women).

'TRADITIONAL' EXPECTATIONS FOR GIRLS

To cry if hurt

To be gentle, well-behaved and polite

To like dolls and teddy bears, etc.

To play quietly

To dress in pink / frilly 'girly' clothes

To be neat, clean and tidy

'TRADITIONAL' EXPECTATIONS FOR BOYS

To be physical, active, noisy and boisterous

To play with cars and lego

To get dirty and grubby

To be dressed in 'boy' clothes

To be brave if hurt

Culture

Human behaviour which is learned from the family and wider society is known as CULTURE.

Traditions • Family size • Religion • Language & dialect • Music, songs, drama, literature & art • Education • Food • Hygiene

A S P E C T S   O F   C U L T U R E

Religion determines rules of behaviour, provides for worship and celebrations, and influences style of dress and diet. In a multicultural society, such as Britain, there are many different ETHNIC GROUPS, each with their own special culture.

Socialisation

Newborn babies are completely dependent on others if they are to survive, grow and develop. Their basic needs are first met by their parents, who also have a key role in teaching them what is expected of them (PRIMARY SOCIALISATION). Later they will be influenced by the society in which they live (SECONDARY SOCIALISATION).

A family must provide children with...

- suitable clothing for the climate
- suitable warmth and shelter
- safe environment
- food and drink to enable them to grow and be healthy
- money to provide basic needs, books, toys, etc.
- appropriate health care
- secure and stable environment
- physical care
- opportunities for learning and developing
- socialisation skills
- training and discipline

- encouragement and praise to develop self-esteem and confidence
- love, affection, comfort, companionship and friendship
- good role models
- reasonable expectations for their age
- communication skills.

Deciding to Have a Baby

Improved and easily accessible contraception means that couples have choices and can plan when to have or not have children. Before having a child it is vitally important that couples discuss their feelings with each other in an honest and open way, consider the number of children they would like, and reach some agreement on the way in which they will be raised. Having a baby has a profound and permanent effect on the parents' lives.

Considerations Before Having a Child

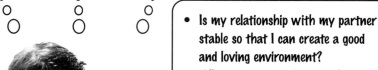

- Is where I live big enough for an extra person?
- Can I afford the cost of equipment, clothing, food, etc.

- Can I cope with lack of sleep and altered sleep patterns?
- Am I fit, active and healthy enough to be a parent?

- Am I too young or too old to be a parent?
- Am I mature enough for the long-lasting responsibility that a child will bring?

- Will I still be able to have an active social life, go on holiday, pursue my hobbies?
- Am I willing to change my lifestyle to accommodate the needs of a child?
- Who will babysit if I go out?

- Is my relationship with my partner stable so that I can create a good and loving environment?
- What support can I expect from my family and friends?

- Have I done all the things I want to do or will I resent my child for restricting my freedom?
- Do I have realistic expectations of children?

- Will my job prospects be affected if I have a career break?
- Do I want to stay at home and look after my child?
- Who will look after my child if I return to work?

The positive side of being a parent is that a child can be a source of great joy and pride. The pleasure of raising it can be a joint venture, which brings immense satisfaction and love to a relationship.

Bad Reasons for Having a Baby

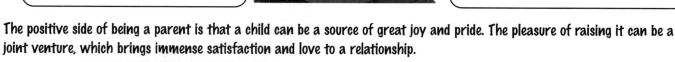

To have someone to 'look after' or 'love'. Babies are a lifelong commitment and make many demands.

To help improve a poor or difficult relationship with your partner – having a baby usually has the opposite effect.

Family pressure – parents cannot wait to be grandparents and keep asking when it will happen or drop hints about this.

To have someone who will love you.

Peer pressure – because your friends have children you think you should too, so you will not feel left out.

To prove you are 'grown up'.

So that you can leave a job you do not like.

A woman's biological clock is ticking and she fears if she does not have a baby soon it may not be possible in the future.

Babies which are not planned are not necessarily 'unwanted'. Most have very good parents, who love them 'to bits'.

The Male Reproductive System

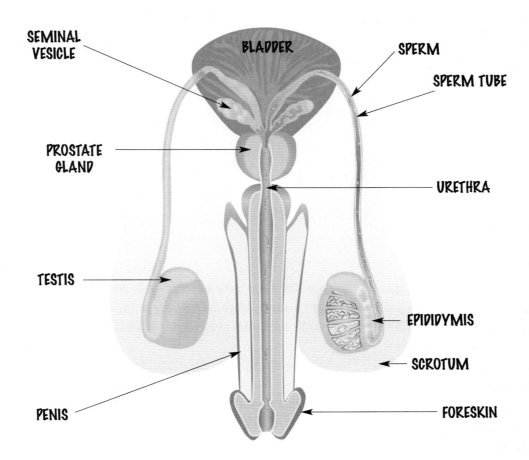

SEMINAL VESICLE

BLADDER

SPERM

SPERM TUBE

PROSTATE GLAND

URETHRA

TESTIS

EPIDIDYMIS

SCROTUM

PENIS

FORESKIN

TESTIS - This produces sperm and the hormone TESTOSTERONE

SCROTUM - This is a bag of skin which contains the two testes. It hangs outside the body which allows sperm to be stored at a lower temperature than body heat i.e. 35°C

SPERM TUBE (VAS DEFERENS) - Sperm travel through this from the testes to the urethra.

PROSTATE GLAND AND SEMINAL VESICLES - These glands add fluid to the sperm to form SEMEN. This fluid activates the sperm and provides energy for it.

URETHRA - This tube transports semen and urine out of the body. During intercourse the exit from the bladder is closed so there is no possibility of these two fluids mixing.

PENIS - This varies in length in different males. It is limp, except when sexually stimulated, when it will fill with blood and become hard (ERECTION). It ejaculates semen into the vagina and then becomes flaccid (i.e. limp).

FORESKIN - This covers and protects the end of the penis. It is sometimes surgically removed for medical or religious reasons. This is called CIRCUMCISION.

Production and Release of Sperm

Sperm is produced by the testes and stored at the beginning of the sperm duct in a region called the EPIDIDYMIS. When ejaculation takes place, sperm is released and rushes through the ducts. As it passes along the ducts, the PROSTATE GLAND and the SEMINAL VESICLES release seminal fluid which nourishes the sperm. The mixture of sperm and seminal fluid is a milky white fluid referred to as SEMEN.

The Female Reproductive System

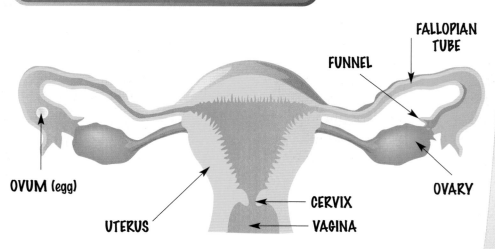

FALLOPIAN TUBE

FUNNEL

OVUM (egg)

UTERUS

CERVIX

VAGINA

OVARY

DID YOU KNOW?
...that a baby girl is born with a store of eggs already present in her ovaries? These start to be released at puberty, but decrease in quality as the woman ages making conception more difficult. After the MENOPAUSE it is no longer possible to become pregnant naturally. With assisted conception women in their late 60s have given birth.

UTERUS - A pear-shaped organ the size of a clenched fist. It has very muscular walls and enlarges during pregnancy. It weighs approximately 30g normally and in a pregnant woman, approximately 1kg at the time of birth.

LINING OF THE UTERUS (ENDOMETRIUM) - Each month this comes away during MENSTRUATION (PERIOD) if a fertilized ovum (EGG) has not been implanted in it.

FALLOPIAN TUBE (OVIDUCT OR EGG TUBE) - This links the ovaries with the uterus. Fertilization takes place here after the sperm and the egg join.

FUNNEL - This catches the ova when it has been released and wafts it into the fallopian tube.

OVARIES - Ova (eggs) are produced and once a month are released, usually from one ovary only, though sometimes from both. This is called OVULATION. Ovaries help to control the levels of female sex hormones OESTROGEN and PROGESTERONE in the body and are responsible for the onset of PUBERTY (at sometime between 10 and 14 years).

VAGINA - This is 10-12cm long and leads from the outside of the body to the cervix. Sperm are deposited at the top of the vagina during intercourse.

CERVIX - This is a strong ring of muscle at the neck of the uterus. It has a very small opening to allow menstrual blood and semen to pass through it.

The Menstrual Cycle

The function of the menstrual cycle is to release an egg and prepare the uterus to receive it if it is fertilised. This is illustrated below:

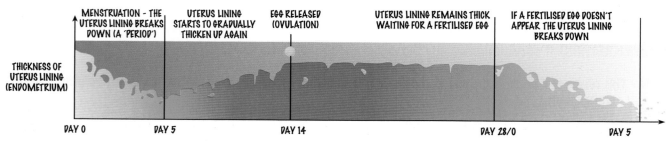

THICKNESS OF UTERUS LINING (ENDOMETRIUM)

MENSTRUATION - THE UTERUS LINING BREAKS DOWN (A 'PERIOD')

UTERUS LINING STARTS TO GRADUALLY THICKEN UP AGAIN

EGG RELEASED (OVULATION)

UTERUS LINING REMAINS THICK WAITING FOR A FERTILISED EGG

IF A FERTILISED EGG DOESN'T APPEAR THE UTERUS LINING BREAKS DOWN

DAY 0   DAY 5   DAY 14   DAY 28/0   DAY 5

REMEMBER THE CYCLE CAN VARY ENORMOUSLY FROM PERSON TO PERSON AND MONTH TO MONTH DUE TO FACTORS SUCH AS STRESS, DIET, HEALTH, AGE, ETC.

Preventing Pregnancy

'Contraception' is the word used to describe the deliberate prevention of pregnancy. Its basic aim is to either   a) prevent the egg and sperm from meeting so that fertilisation cannot take place.

or   b) prevent implantation of a fertilised egg into the uterus.

Without contraception most sexually active women will become pregnant within a year. Contraception has been practised throughout history, e.g. the Egyptians used a mixture containing crocodile dung, which they placed in the vagina. Nowadays contraceptives are much more reliable and advice may be obtained from GPs, Family Planning Clinics, Well-women Clinics, the Brooke Advisory Service, chemists, Youth Centres, etc. Under 16's don't need parental consent but will be actively encouraged to speak to their parents about contraception. Despite this it is estimated that 1 in 3 pregnancies are unplanned.

NB:
- ALL contraception must be correctly used if it is to be effective.
- The contraception chosen by couples will depend on their personal preference, religious beliefs, age and whether a long- or short-term method is needed.

The Myths

Many myths and false beliefs surround getting pregnant. Remember...

... A WOMAN <u>CAN</u> GET PREGNANT EVEN IF...

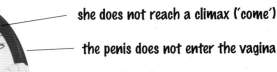

she is breast-feeding a child —   — she does not reach a climax ('come')

intercourse takes place during a period —   — the penis does not enter the vagina

the vagina is douched (washed out) after intercourse —   — she has not yet had a period

— it is the first time she has had intercourse

Natural Family Planning

Natural family planning identifies fertile and infertile times in the menstrual cycle so that intercourse can be timed to reduce the possibility of pregnancy; both partners must be committed to this, trained in its use and understand how it works. The benefits of natural family planning is that no chemical or physical intervention is used, there are no side effects and all cultures, faiths and religions find it acceptable. However, these methods are UNRELIABLE particularly if periods are irregular or the woman is ill. Also very careful daily records must be kept and intercourse must be avoided during the fertile period. The four different methods are based on the following criteria:

i) <u>CERVICAL MUCUS</u> – This changes in texture and amount at different times in the menstrual cycle.

ii) <u>TEMPERATURE METHOD</u> – The body temperature rises after ovulation.

iii) <u>CALENDAR METHOD</u> – Uses the length of the menstrual cycle.

iv) <u>PERSONA</u> (Computerised menstrual cycle monitor) – Monitors changes in temperature, urine and saliva.

EMERGENCY CONTRACEPTION

These should be used only when other methods of contraception have failed.
1) 'The Morning After Pill' prescribed by doctors and available at some chemists over the counter. They must be taken within 72 hours of unprotected sexual intercourse, according to the instructions. They prevent implantation (or delay ovulation).
2) An I.U.D. inserted by a doctor within 5 days of unprotected sexual intercourse would also prevent a pregnancy occurring.

Withdrawal Method

The withdrawal method (coitus interuptus) or 'being careful' involves the penis being removed before ejaculation so that no sperm are placed in the vagina. This method is very unreliable as semen may leak from the penis before ejaculation or the man may get 'carried away'. People who find other methods unacceptable tend to use this method.

Abstention

Abstention or saying 'no' is 100% reliable: there is no intercourse so there is no possibility of the sperm and egg meeting.

Contraception Methods Available Through Chemists And Doctors

METHOD	% EFFECTIVE DUTY OF ...	HOW IT WORKS	ADVANTAGES	DISADVANTAGES
Male Condom	98% ♂	Sperm are prevented from entering the vagina.	• Free from Family Planning Clinics • Widely available in chemists, supermarkets, clubs, etc. • Protects both partners from STIs (Sexually Transmitted Infections) including AIDS.	• It may split, be damaged or slip off • It must be put on correctly, onto an erect penis • Putting it on can interrupt sexual intercourse • The man must withdraw quickly after ejaculation
Female Condom (Femidom)	95% ♀	As above	• Protects both partners from STIs (including AIDS)	• Expensive to buy • The penis must be placed to enter the condom and not positioned between the condom and the vagina
Diaphragm (cap) with spermicide (jelly or cream)	92–96% ♀	Prevents sperm from meeting an egg by providing a barrier. Sperm are made inactive by spermicide	• No health risks from side effects • A wide variety to choose from	• Must stay in place 6 hours after intercourse • Must be fitted by a doctor and checked every 12 months for size • Bladder infections may be a side effect
I.U.D. (Intrauterine device)	98–99% ♀	Prevents implantation of a fertilised egg	• Works immediately once fitted • Can remain in place for a long time (3–10 years)	• May cause heavier, longer or more painful periods • Not suitable for all women • Must be inserted by a doctor • Sometimes comes out
I.U.S. (Intrauterine system)	99%+ ♀	Progestogen is slowly released preventing sperm from meeting an egg	• Works immediately when inserted • Prevents pregnancy for 5 years • Periods are lighter and shorter	• Irregular light bleeding is possible in the first 3 months • Must be inserted by a doctor • Acne and tender breasts are possible side effects
Combined Pill (Contains oestrogen and progestogen)	100% ♀	Prevents ovaries from producing eggs	• Easily taken orally	• Vomiting, diarrhoea and antibiotics make it become unreliable • If taken 12 hours late it becomes unreliable • Must be prescribed by a doctor • Best avoided by women who smoke
Mini-pill (P.O.P.) (Contains progestogen only)	99% ♀	Makes it difficult for sperm to enter the uterus and / or implantation of fertilized ovum.	• Easily taken orally • Can relieve PMT and painful periods	• If taken more than 3 hours late it becomes unreliable • Vomiting and diarrhoea make it become unreliable • Must be prescribed by a doctor
Contraceptive implant (slow release progestogen)	99% ♀	Prevents egg and sperm meeting and / or implantation.	• Effective for up to 3 years • Fertility returns immediately when implant is removed	• Can be difficult to remove • Side effects include excessive or irregular bleeding
Contraceptive injection (progestogen)	99% ♀	Makes it difficult for sperm to enter the uterus and for fertilized egg to implant	• Effective for 2/3 months	• Possible side effects include irregular bleeding • There is no antidote if the woman changes her mind • Must be given by a doctor

Sterilisation

Neither male nor female sterilisation affects sexual intercourse, they are both permanent and once established as being successful no other contraception is needed. They are 99.5% effective.

FEMALE: During a hospital operation the fallopian tubes are cut or blocked preventing sperm and egg meeting. This is permanent, though it is worth remembering that they can sometimes become unblocked or rejoined. It is effective following the first period after the operation.

MALE: This is a relatively minor operation in which the sperm tube (vas deferens) is cut or blocked using rings or clips, thus preventing sperm from passing through. Once two negative sperm tests have been done the operation will be considered successful though, as with female sterilisation, the tubes can sometimes rejoin. It is not easy to reverse if the man changes his mind.

Conception

In order to become pregnant an egg must be fertilised by a sperm.

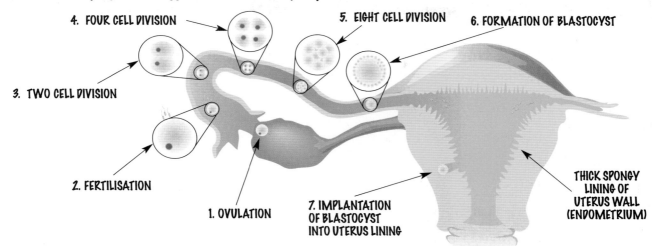

4. FOUR CELL DIVISION

5. EIGHT CELL DIVISION

6. FORMATION OF BLASTOCYST

3. TWO CELL DIVISION

2. FERTILISATION

1. OVULATION

7. IMPLANTATION OF BLASTOCYST INTO UTERUS LINING

THICK SPONGY LINING OF UTERUS WALL (ENDOMETRIUM)

When ejaculated from the penis the sperm swim from the vagina, through the cervix, into the uterus and along the fallopian tube. It only takes one sperm to FERTILISE an egg (CONCEPTION). The sperm and the egg fuse and become one cell. This cell divides and continues to divide to produce a BLASTOCYST. This travels down the fallopian tube and into the uterus. Here, if the uterus lining is ready, IMPLANTATION will occur approximately 4-6 days after fertilisation and the blastocyst will develop into an embryo.

When conception occurs changes in the levels of oestrogen and progesterone cause the blood vessel-rich lining of the uterus to be maintained so that the developing embryo can be supplied with food and oxygen after implantation.

Basic Genetics

Genes are inherited from both parents and determine the characteristics of a person. Thousands of genes together form chromosomes which carry the information the body needs to grow and develop. Genes can be DOMINANT (STRONG) or RECESSIVE (WEAK) and it is this factor that influences the inheritance of a characteristic, e.g. body shape, hair texture, skin colour, from either the mother or father. There are 46 chromosomes in every cell in the body, except for the sperm and ova (the sex cells), which contain 23 each. However, at conception, these become one cell which will then also contain 46 chromosomes.

SPERM 23

OVUM 23 → CONCEPTION → 46 → DIVISION → 46 46 → DIVISION → 46 46 / 46 46 → DIVISION → 46 46 46 46 46 46 46 46

Faulty genes can cause inherited diseases, as can the presence of an extra chromosome. Down's syndrome is caused by having a specific extra chromosome, i.e. 47, whereas Turner's Syndrome is caused when baby girls have only one X chromosome, i.e. 45 in total.

The Inheritance Of Sex

The sex of a baby is determined by the sex chromosomes present in the egg and sperm.

- All eggs contain one X chromosome.
- A sperm may contain an X chromosome or a Y chromosome.
- The sex of the child depends on which type of sperm fertilises the egg.

What It Is

Pre-conceptual care takes place BEFORE PLANNED CONCEPTION. A woman may choose to have this care from her GP, Practice Nurse or Family Planning Clinic in order to gain optimum health benefits for herself and her baby.

The Checklist

ALCOHOL	Should be avoided
SMOKING	Should be stopped. Avoid passive smoking from smoky atmospheres.
RECREATIONAL DRUGS	Groups are available to support users of illegal substances wishing to give up.
STIs (Sexually Transmitted Infections)	Should be checked for chlamydia and other STIs including gonorrhoea, syphilis, HIV, Hepatitis B. They can all affect fertility.
IMMUNITY	Immunity to rubella and polio should be checked.
EXERCISE	Should be taken regularly.
CONTRACEPTION	Discuss stopping contraception and the implications, e.g. stop taking the pill, remove I.U.D.
DIET	Eat a healthy diet, especially one rich in folic acid. Take folic acid supplements for 3 months before conception to prevent spina bifida
MEDICATIONS	Medications taken for epilepsy, kidney disease, diabetes, heart disease, etc. may need adjusting so that the condition can continue to be treated without harming the baby. Discuss with the GP.
FATHERS	Fathers also need to be healthy to produce good quality sperm. They should give up smoking, drinking alcohol and eat a healthy diet. Not only will this support and encourage their partners but it will improve their own wellbeing

INTERESTING FACT

Marijuana affects sperm production for 3-9 months after it is last used

Genetic Counselling

Couples who need specific advice about the risk of passing on inherited diseases can be tested to give them an accurate indication of the likelihood of them having an affected child. Such diseases include cystic fibrosis, haemophilia, thalassaemia, PKU and muscular dystrophy. Some genetic diseases, e.g. haemophilia are only found in males. Females, although not affected, can pass the condition on to their sons.

Common Causes Of Infertility

Infertility is the inability to conceive (women) or father children (men). It affects one in ten couples. The problem may lie with the woman, or the man, or both. Couples can obtain advice from the GP or Family Planning Clinic. If the remedy is not straightforward they will be referred to a specialist for investigation and assistance. In the past many couples had to remain childless, but now, with modern technology, they can be helped. However, as technology advances moral and ethical issues are raised and new laws sometimes have to be introduced to deal with these.

CAUSES OF INFERTILITY

NOT ENOUGH SPERM...
If a man has a low sperm count conception is difficult. 20 000 000 are needed in each ejaculation for an ova to be fertilised. Lack of sperm can be a result of medical conditions or having contracted mumps after the age of 12.

HYSTERECTOMY...
The uterus is surgically removed so there is nowhere for the foetus to grow and develop

THICK CERVICAL MUCUS...
This prevents sperm from reaching the fallopian tubes.

BLOCKED FALLOPIAN TUBES...
This prevents sperm from reaching the ova. It may be a result of endometriosis or an infection such as chlamydia. Surgery can sometimes repair the damage.

CANCER TREATMENT...
This can leave men and women infertile. Prior to chemotherapy they are often offered the option of their eggs or sperm being collected and stored for later use.

OVULATION DOES NOT TAKE PLACE...
This means there are no eggs to be fertilised. It may only be a short-term problem caused by hormonal contraceptive devices or it could be more serious. Hormones (fertility drugs) can be given to stimulate the ovaries into producing eggs. When they are prescribed extreme caution is used to try to avoid multiple births. In many cases no cause is found, therefore IVF used.

Treatment Of Infertility (Assisted Conception)

IVF (*In Vitro* Fertilisation)
Sometimes this is known as having a 'test-tube' baby because fertilisation of the egg takes place in the laboratory. A woman is given hormone treatment to stimulate egg production and then monitored closely so that the eggs can be 'surgically harvested' (removed by an operation). Sperm are then introduced and penetrate the ovum. They are observed through a microscope for cell division. At 8-cell-division stage they are selected and up to 3 are replaced in the uterus. If they are replaced in the fallopian tube this is known as GIFT (Gamete Intra-Fallopian Transfer).

DONOR INSEMINATION (DI)
Sperm from a donor is used either for DI (placed directly into the uterus) or IVF treatment.

ARTIFICIAL INSEMINATION BY HUSBAND (AIH)
This places sperm directly into the uterus to avoid hostile cervical mucus.

ICSI (Intra-cytoplasmic Sperm Injection)
Sometimes sperm are not able to penetrate the ovum. In order to enable fertilisation to take place selected sperm are injected directly into the ovum in the laboratory. As with IVF, at 8-cell division stage they are transferred to the uterus or fallopian tubes. Any fertilised ovum which are not needed can be frozen for future use by the parents. Alternatively, they can be donated to another couple with parental permission (EMBRYO DONATION).

SURROGACY
For some infertile couples this can be an option. Another woman will offer to incubate a baby in her uterus and then hand it over at birth. The husband's sperm can be used to fertilise the surrogate's egg using artificial insemination.

EGG DONATION
If a woman is unable to produce eggs she is reliant upon an egg donor so that she can then use the IVF procedure. Donor women's ovaries will be stimulated to produce many eggs which are harvested when mature and then allocated to suitable women.

PGD (Pre-implantation Genetic Diagnosis)
This is used by couples who have been identified as being carriers of a serious genetic disorder. IVF takes place but then embryos are checked to make sure that they do not have the disorder. Only healthy embryos are used.

All the above procedures are available through the National Health Service and the private sector. There is much regional variation in provision and waiting lists can be lengthy.

This is where more than one foetus develops in the uterus. This can occur naturally. If fertility treatment is used then there is an increased probability of a multiple pregnancy.

Identical Twins (Uniovular Twins)

If a fertilised egg splits completely into two parts then each part develops into a separate baby. Identical twins have identical genes so will look the same, i.e. same hair colour, eye colour, facial features. They will have the same blood group and will be the same sex. In the uterus they will share the same placenta. Young mothers are more likely to have identical twins than older mothers.

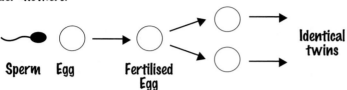

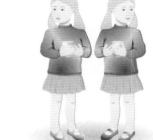

Sperm Egg Fertilised Egg Identical twins

Conjoined Twins

If a fertilised egg splits partially into two, then CONJOINED twins will result. Conjoined twins are very rare. Vital organs may be shared which makes surgical separation an extremely difficult procedure to undertake. In some instances shared organs can be divided, e.g. liver. Sometimes the babies are only superficially joined, e.g. at the chest. In this case surgery can be successful and enable the babies to lead separate and independent lives.

Non-identical Twins (Binovular Or Fraternal Twins)

If two eggs are released at the same time and fertilised by two separate sperm then two babies will result. They will be no more alike than any other siblings. Biologically they will be different as they will have different genes.

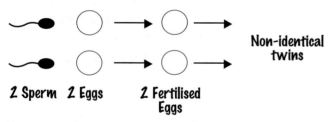

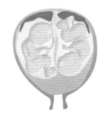

Non-identical twins

2 Sperm 2 Eggs 2 Fertilised Eggs

If a woman has unprotected sex with more than one sexual partner within a very short space of time it is possible that her fraternal twins could be conceived by two different fathers. Non-identical twins have their own individual placentas and may be different sexes. They are most likely to be born to older mothers and to those who have had previous pregnancies. They are also more likely to be born to a family with a history of twins.

Possible Complications With Multiple Pregnancies

- With a multiple pregnancy it is likely that labour will begin prematurely.
- Twins are often smaller than average weight at birth. The larger the number of babies the less each baby will generally weigh.
- Ante-natal check up will be required more often than normal to check for potential complications.
- It is possible that a Caesarean Section MAY be needed for a twin birth; more than two babies are always delivered by Caesarean Section.
- There is an increased incidence of congenital abnormalities.

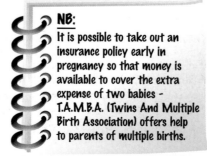

NB:
It is possible to take out an insurance policy early in pregnancy so that money is available to cover the extra expense of two babies - T.A.M.B.A. (Twins And Multiple Birth Association) offers help to parents of multiple births.

Two babies = Twins
Three babies = Triplets
Four babies = Quads (Quadruplets)
Five babies = Quins (Quintuplets)
Six babies = Sextuplets

Possible Indications Of Early Pregnancy

Pregnancy may be indicated by some or all of the following. However, they are not conclusive evidence and may have other causes!

- Constipation
- More frequent need to urinate
- Feeling exhausted, dizzy or faint
- Enlarged tender breasts with more obvious blue veins. Nipples and areola go dark pink/brown
- Missed period
- Increased vaginal discharge
- Odd metallic taste in the mouth
- Sudden dislike or aversion to previously enjoyed food and drink, e.g. coffee
- Sickness or nausea, usually in the morning ('morning sickness'), but not always; it can occur at any time.

Pregnancy Testing

Free tests carried out by a GP, Brook Advisory Service, Family Planning Clinic or the British Pregnancy Advisory Service can confirm a pregnancy. The most common way in which women establish that they are pregnant is by using a HOME PREGNANCY TESTING kit. These can be bought for under £10 at chemists and supermarkets. They can be used in private from the day on which a period is due. They give a result in minutes. Instructions for different tests vary slightly and must be followed carefully to obtain an accurate result. An absorbent sampler is placed into a specimen of mid-stream urine to check for the presence of the hormone GONADOTROPHIN. The results are displayed in a window on the sample stick. When a pregnancy is confirmed a woman should see her GP, Practice Nurse or Midwife at her local clinic to arrange for a plan of care. This will start with a 'booking-in' appointment.

NB A positive pregnancy test is very rarely wrong. However, a negative test should be re-done after two weeks because low levels of the hormone at an early stage do not always register.

EDD (Estimated Delivery Date)

Because all the calculations used are based on a 28-day cycle this date is an 'estimated' date. Some babies arrive before their EDD, some after. An average length of pregnancy is 40 weeks but 38-42 is normal. To estimate the EDD...

   a) add 9 months and 7 days to the first day of the last period
or b) count 280 days from the first day of the last period.

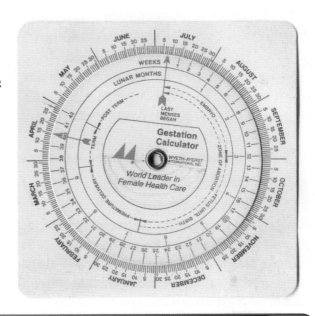

NB Because conception takes place on day 14 of the cycle, week 8 of a pregnancy is actually only 6 weeks after conception. A much more reliable indication of the EDD can be obtained from an early dating scan, especially as some women experience light bleeding in the first month, which they mistake for a period. Special charts make calculating the EDD easier.

Miscarriage (Early and Late)

When a baby is expelled from the uterus (born) before it is VIABLE (able to survive on its own) it is called a miscarriage. A baby is classed as viable at 24 weeks gestation or above. If the baby is born dead after 24 weeks this is called a STILLBIRTH. It is estimated that 1 in 3 women miscarry a baby but then go on to have further normal pregnancies and produce healthy babies. Some early miscarriages go almost unnoticed and may be regarded as a late heavy period. Most occur in the first 12-14 weeks of pregnancy usually because the baby or the placenta is failing to develop normally.

POSSIBLE PROBLEMS	DESCRIPTION
Threatened miscarriage	There is bleeding from the vagina but the foetus is not expelled from the uterus. This may result in a miscarriage or the pregnancy may continue normally.
Early or late miscarriage	The foetus is expelled naturally by the body through the vagina.
Silent miscarriage	The foetus dies in utero but is not spontaneously expelled. It is often discovered during a scan and must be removed with medical assistance either by inducing labour or by a D and C (dilation and curettage).

Signs And Symptoms Of Miscarriage

The following signs may indicate a miscarriage...
- Vaginal bleeding - heavy bleeding from the vagina which does not stop
  - blood spots accompanied by severe abdominal pain **NB** Light bleeding and blood spotting can occur in a normal pregnancy.
- Cramp-like period pains.
- Clear or pink fluid leaking from the vagina is likely to be amniotic fluid from inside a ruptured amniotic sac.

The causes of miscarriage will only normally be investigated further in women who have experienced 3 in succession. If the causes can be identified then it may be possible to deal with them. Also, whilst some causes are relatively easy to identify (see below), that is not always the case.

> Easily identifiable causes of miscarriage include...
> - Severe maternal infection, e.g. toxoplasmosis
> - Insufficient hormone levels, especially progesterone
> - Auto-immune disease in the mother whose body rejects the foetus
> - Cervical incompetence
> - Fibroids (small growths in the uterus)
> - Foetal abnormalities
>   - chromosomal
>   - major developmental
> - Exposure to toxins, e.g. radiation, chemotherapy drugs
> - A malformed uterus

NB After a miscarriage an ultrasound scan may be done to check that all the products of conception have been expelled.

A-Z Of Minor Problems

Midwives and GPs can often suggest or prescribe remedies to alleviate the symptoms of minor problems. These can occur at different times throughout the pregnancy and are listed below.
Backache, breathlessness, constipation, cramp, dental problems, feeling faint, flushing, frequent urination, heartburn, nausea, numbness, piles, sickness, sweating, swollen ankles, thrush, tiredness, inability to sleep, urine leakage, varicose veins.
However, in many cases women positively 'glow' during pregnancy, and have relatively few problems.

ALCOHOL – Avoid all alcohol because it can pass from the mother's bloodstream through the placenta to the baby. Drinking alcohol during pregnancy INCREASES THE RISK to the baby of Foetal Alcohol Syndrome. This increases the risk of mental retardation, retarded growth, stillbirth and damage to the central nervous system.

ANIMALS – CHLAMYDIOSIS from close contact with lambs or their mothers can cause miscarriage.
TOXOPLASMOSIS from cat faeces can cause miscarriage, stillbirth or blindness in the baby. Litter trays should always be emptied using gloves.

AROMATHERAPY – Some essential oils may cause miscarriage, however others can be used to help minimise discomfort from backache, swollen legs and ankles and nausea.

CLOTHES – During pregnancy the abdomen gets bigger so CLOTHES must either be loose or expandable around the waist. Some are designed with adjustable fastenings or built-in 'growing room' to allow for expansion. Many women simply buy baggier clothes in larger sizes to accommodate their 'bump'. The days when pregnancy was hidden have disappeared and modern, stretch fabrics which emphasise the figure are chosen by some women. Good-fitting bras which offer support to the breasts are important. They should be correctly fitted, not squash the nipple, and have wide straps for comfort.
LOW- OR MEDIUM-HEELED SHOES prevent backache and help the mother retain her balance.

DRUGS – Most drugs can cross the placenta and may harm the foetus or cause withdrawal symptoms when the baby is born.
ILLEGAL DRUGS (RECREATIONAL) – Examples are LSD, tranquilizers, cannabis, Ecstasy, heroin, amphetamines and the fumes from solvents such as glue and aerosol gasses. They cause withdrawal symptoms in the babies after birth. Drug addicted babies are typically smaller than average, irritable and much more difficult to settle. Many have a characteristic high-pitched cry. All will require admission to a SCBU (see page 36). They may be mentally impaired and have lifelong problems.
PRESCRIBED DRUGS If the mother is taking prescribed drugs for a pre-existing condition such as diabetes the GP should be informed of her pregnancy so that the foetus is not harmed. Over-the-counter medicines such as travel sickness pills and some indigestion remedies can be damaging to the foetus. No medicines should be taken during pregnancy without the advice of the GP, midwife or pharmacist.

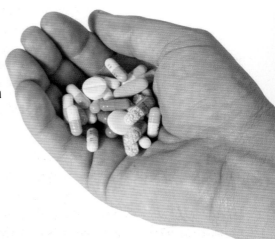

XERCISE – Being pregnant should not interfere with a woman's normal exercise regime. Activities such as aerobics, walking, swimming, dance classes and cycling can be continued until birth unless they become uncomfortable. It would be unwise to ski or do high-risk activities such as hang-gliding! If exercise has not been part of a woman's routine before pregnancy she should check with her midwife about starting to exercise gradually.

The benefits of exercise are that it...

- Provides social activity
- Aids sleep
- Builds and tones muscles
- Controls weight gain
- Makes labour easier
- Helps figure return to pre-pregnancy shape quicker after birth.

AQUA-NATAL CLASSES are held in swimming pools at quieter times. They are organised by obstetric physiotherapists or midwives.

AQUA-ROBIC CLASSES can be continued as normal if the mother advises the instructor of her pregnancy and modifies her programme.

OOD – See pages 43, 44 and 45.
Some foods should be avoided during pregnancy. See chart below.

FOODS TO AVOID	PROBLEM	SYMPTOMS AND EFFECTS
• Eggs (unless hard-boiled). • Products containing raw egg, e.g. Royal icing	Salmonella	Food poisoning
• Unpasteurised milk or products made from this, e.g. Soft cheese, brie, camembert, stilton • Cook-chill foods (unless reheated thoroughly to 72°C) • Paté • Undercooked meat	Listeriosis	Severe illness, miscarriage, stillbirth baby born with listeriosis (seriously ill)
• Liver and liver products, e.g. liver paté	Vitamin A	Too much vitamin A poisons the baby
• Undercooked meat (beware BBQs) • Fruit and vegetables with soil on	Toxoplasmosis	Miscarriage, stillbirth, baby born blind
• Peanuts and products containing peanuts	Peanut allergy can be passed on to the baby	Allergic reaction in a child can cause death

YGIENE – Food hygiene and personal hygiene is of utmost importance because infections such as toxoplasmosis can cause miscarriage.

NFECTIOUS DISEASES – Minor infections cannot be avoided in everyday life and do not harm the baby Contact with RUBELLA (GERMAN MEASLES) and CHICKEN POX should be avoided especially in the first 3-4 months of pregnancy.

PELVIC FLOOR EXERCISES – The muscles around the vagina, bowel and bladder openings need to be strengthened to cope with the strain of pregnancy and birth. This can be done by exercising them. Details of how to do this will be taught by the midwife.

POSTURE – If a pregnant woman stands and sits with her weight evenly balanced her posture will be good. It can take time to adjust to carrying the extra weight in pregnancy but good posture will avoid backache. When bending over or lifting she should bend from the knees or kneel to avoid strain.

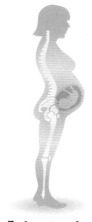

Good posture before pregnancy

Bad posture in pregnancy, which may cause backache

Good posture in pregnancy

REST AND RELAXATION – This is important especially in the last 3 months. The mother should aim to rest for an hour a day as this can prevent backache and varicose veins. Relaxation helps to reduce stress so the mother should do any activity that she enjoys to aid this.

SLEEP – At the beginning of pregnancy a mother should sleep as much as she can as she may well feel unusually tired. After 23 weeks her sleep may be disturbed by the baby kicking or by a need to urinate more often because the baby is pressing on her bladder. Her change in shape may make it more difficult to get comfortable and she may get support by using extra pillows.

SMOKING – Chemicals from cigarette smoke pass to the baby from the mother's blood via the placenta. One of these, NICOTINE, increases the baby's heartbeat. The other, CARBON MONOXIDE, decreases its oxygen level which affects its growth and development.
Passive smoking is equally damaging.
Smoking increases the risk of...

- premature birth
- lower than average birth weight (by an average of 200g)
- miscarriage, stillbirth or death in the first week, SIDS
- foetal abnormalities
- damage to the placenta
- learning difficulties in later life

Children born to heavy smokers or who live in a smoky home are much more prone to bronchitis, pneumonia and other chest infections.

TEETH – Dental treatment is free during pregnancy and for the 12 months following the birth. Mothers should have regular checkups as the gums may need extra attention and tooth decay is more likely to occur.

X-RAYS – X-rays can damage the baby in utero and so should be avoided. The dentist needs to be informed of pregnancy so that a mother-to-be is not exposed to a dental x-ray.

Week 6 (4 Weeks After Conception)

The EMBRYO is about the size of a grain of rice 4-6mm ($\frac{1}{4}$") and floats in a sac of fluid. Its heart is beating. Initial development of the arms, legs, brain, spine, cerebral nervous system, internal organs, blood, bones, muscle, ears and eyes has begun.

Actual size: ⊢⊣

Week 8 (6 Weeks After Conception)

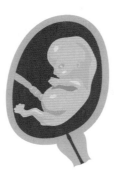

The embryo has begun to look more human and is now known as a FOETUS. It is 2.2cm (1") long measured from crown to rump (head to bottom). That is about as big as a strawberry. It can move around in the amniotic sac. The heart has valves and the heartbeat is visible on an ultrasound scan. The main organs are further developed and are all present in a basic form. Arms, legs and shoulders are visible. The ears and eyes are forming.

Actual size: ⊢————⊣

Week 12 (10 Weeks After Conception)

The foetus is now fully formed. It is 6cm (2.5") from crown to rump and about as big as a mouse. Its heart beats strongly. It can swim and move, turning its head and kicking but these movements are not felt by the mother yet. The sex organs are well developed as are muscles, nerves, organs, limbs and bones. The foetus can now swallow, clench a fist, frown, hiccup and suck a thumb. It is sensitive to heat, light and sound. The eyes remain closed.

NB The placenta is now fully formed.

Actual size: ⊢—————————⊣

Week 24

The foetus is 21cm (8") long and weighs 700g (1.5lbs). It is covered with VERNIX and LANUGO (see page 38). Its face is fully formed but the eyes will not open for another 2 weeks. It has hair and red, wrinkled skin. It moves a lot and has periods of waking and sleeping. The bones are starting to harden. It has soft nails and fingerprints.

If the baby was born now it would have a reasonable chance of survival as its development is almost complete. It would need care in a NEONATAL INTENSIVE CARE UNIT (NICU) or SPECIAL CARE BABY UNIT (SCBU) because its lungs would not be working and it would require help with breathing. In the last few weeks the baby has to grow (its length will double), get stronger and triple its weight as fat is deposited under the skin.

Week 36

By 32-36 weeks the baby is usually lying head downwards. This is called the CEPHALIC position.

The CEPHALIC Position

The baby will remain in this position (see right) until birth. If the baby doesn't assume this position it may be in the breech position and then the birth can be complicated and medical intervention may be needed.

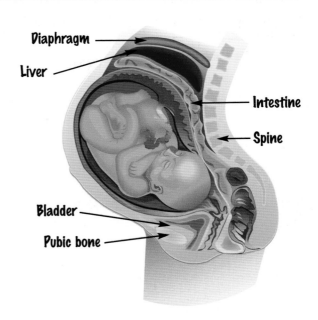

Diaphragm
Liver
Intestine
Spine
Bladder
Pubic bone

Ectopic Pregnancy

If a fertilised egg implants itself in the fallopian tube, or some other part of the abdomen, instead of the uterus and continues to grow and develop there then it is called an ECTOPIC pregnancy. It can be extremely dangerous for the mother and baby. In most cases an operation will be performed to remove the foetus, and in many cases remove the fallopian tube.
In a few VERY RARE cases the baby has been able to survive long enough in the wrong place to allow it to be born alive by Caesarean section.

Placenta, Umbilical Cord And Amniotic Sac

In addition to producing an embryo, a fertilised egg also produces a placenta, an umbilical cord and an amniotic sac:

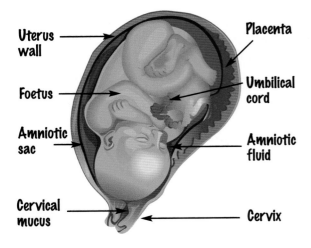

Uterus wall
Placenta
Foetus
Umbilical cord
Amniotic sac
Amniotic fluid
Cervical mucus
Cervix

PLACENTA

The placenta is the only truly disposable organ in the body. It develops to support the baby and is then expelled from the uterus shortly after the baby is born (AFTERBIRTH). It is a large structure made up of soft spongy tissue which, because it is richly supplied with blood, is dark red in colour. When fully grown it is approximately 2.5cm thick, 15cm across and weighs 500g. It is attached to the uterus wall and increases in size with the baby. It provides FOOD and OXYGEN and removes WASTES. These exchanges take place through the blood of the mother and baby which come into close contact but do NOT mix. Antibodies can pass across the placenta as can alcohol, viruses, medicines and nicotine.

AMNIOTIC SAC

The foetus develops in this bag which is filled with amniotic fluid. It is about the size of a dinner plate and weighs about $\frac{1}{8}$ of the baby's weight. The amniotic fluid keeps the baby at a constant temperature of 37°C and, especially in the early stages of pregnancy, the foetus can float freely in it to stretch, flex and exercise the muscles. In here the foetus is cushioned from bangs and knocks, etc. and thus is protected from being damaged.

UMBILICAL CORD

This cord is approximately 50cm long and 2cm wide. It contains 3 blood vessels (2 arteries and 1 vein) which carry blood between the foetus and the mother.

Midwives

A midwife has specialist training to enable her to care for women before, during and after pregnancy.

> The midwife will...
> ... carry out routine testing
> ... offer advice on breast feeding
> ... offer advice on caring for the baby
> ... conduct the 'booking-in' visit
> ... book scans
> ... arrange specialist tests
> ... be qualified to administer some drugs.
>
> They may be either...
> a TEAM MIDWIFE who works as part
> of a professional care team in the
> community
> or...
> a MATERNITY UNIT MIDWIFE who
> works in a hospital.

TEAM MIDWIFE
- Provides ante-natal care for women with straightforward pregnancies.
- Conducts and delivers home and hospital births
- Does selective post-natal visiting for up to 28 days and is available by telephone during this period of time.

MATERNITY UNIT MIDWIFE
- Provides ante-natal care for women with high-risk pregnancies.
- Delivers babies in hospital.
- Looks after mother on ante-natal and post-natal ward.
- Transfers care of mother to team midwife on discharge from hospital.

NB They deliver both straightforward births and those which are more complex such as breech or multiple. They also assist at births which need medical intervention such as Ventouse or Caesarean section.

Other Health Care Professionals

<u>HEALTH VISITORS</u> – These are trained nurses with further specialist Health Visitor qualifications. They will...
- give advice on health matters, feeding, immunisation and any problems.
- keep a check on the child's developmental progress at regular intervals.
- contact the mother ten days after the birth, then visit for up to six weeks or see the mother and baby at her local health centre, where they are based.
- always be available by telephone.
- put the mother in touch with local groups where she can meet and share experiences with other mothers.
- every family with children under 5 has a health visitor.

<u>GPS (GENERAL PRACTITIONERS)</u> – They...
- will have joint responsibility for the mother during pregnancy.
- may visit the mother and baby when they return home from the maternity unit.
- will do the post-natal examination at six weeks.

<u>OBSTETRICIANS</u> – These doctors specialise in caring for women during pregnancy, labour and birth. A consultant obstetrician is responsible for hospital births and will deliver babies where there are complications, e.g. if a Caesarean section is needed, multiple births, breech birth, Ventouse, or forceps.

<u>GYNAECOLOGISTS</u> – They have specialist knowledge about the functions and diseases of the female reproductive system. They may be obstetricians or work closely with one. They treat any problems of the reproductive system and help couples with fertility problems.

<u>PAEDIATRICIANS</u> – They specialise in the care of children. They are responsible for medical checks on babies born in hospital and care for the health of children throughout childhood.

<u>NEO-NATOLOGISTS</u> – They have further specialist training in the care of newborn babies who are in the SCBU (Special Care Baby Unit) because they are premature or need medical treatment.

NB Health care professionals can be male or female.

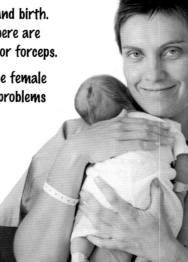

Antenatal Care

Antenatal care is provided by shared care, consultant care and team midwives. Routine tests are carried out and the results of these are compared to those from the 'booking-in' visit, enabling detection of any high-risk conditions, either in the mother or foetus. Foetal growth and the mother's general health are also monitored. Women are allowed, by law, paid time off work to attend antenatal appointments and parentcraft education classes.

During pregnancy a woman gains 10-12.5 kg (22-28lbs) due to the baby, enlarged uterus, placenta, umbilical cord, amniotic fluid and the stored fat which will later be used in milk production. ROUTINE weighing is no longer done.

Frequency And Type Of Standard Check-ups

EXAMINATION OF THE UTERUS – The outside of the abdomen is felt to check the size, position and movement of the foetus. The height of the fundus (distance from the pubic bone to the top of the uterus) is also measured.

First at 8-10 weeks. Then every month until week 28 Then every 2 weeks to week 36 Then every week until delivery (EXCEPT where scheduled visits necessary)

URINE – Is checked for 1) Protein (albumen) which may give an early indication of pre-eclampsia or bladder and kidney infections. 2) Sugar (glucose) may indicate gestational diabetes (disappears after birth) 3) Ketones indicate dehydration / ill health, e.g. vomiting.

CHECKING THE LEGS – These are checked for signs of swelling or varicose veins

BLOOD PRESSURE – Checked using a sphygmomanometer. High blood pressure could indicate PRE-ECLAMPSIA

NB Signs of PRE-ECLAMPSIA include raised blood pressure, protein in the urine, severe headaches, generalised swelling of the body (oedema) and excessive weight gain. It is managed by hospital admission, close monitoring and possible early delivery to prevent the onset of eclampsia. Eclampsia is a very serious condition which can lead to fits, multiple organ failure and maternal and foetal death.

Other Check-ups

FOETAL HEARTBEAT – Checked every visit after 16 weeks using a stethoscope, pinard or hand-held ultrasound scan machine (sonic aid). Normal heartbeat is 110-150 beats per minute.

BLOOD TEST – This is done at 16 weeks and is used to check for 1) Mother's immunity to Rubella (German Measles). 2) Rhesus factor - problems in future pregnancies can be avoided and an injection given if needed. 3) Hepatitis B - treatment can be given to the baby after birth. 4) Diabetes - to check for gestational diabetes. 5) Syphilis - treatment can be given. 6) Mother's blood group - in case a blood transfusion becomes necessary. 7) Anaemia - iron supplements and folic acid may be needed. 8) Tests for HIV status and foetal abnormality will be offered. For which the signed consent of the mother must be given.

ULTRASOUND SCAN – The abdomen is covered with gel to provide good contact and a hand-held scanner is moved slowly over it. Reflected sound waves project an image of the baby, and its internal organs, onto a screen. Information is obtained by taking measurements and observing the images.

EARLY DATING SCAN - This is done before 16 weeks to give an exact age of the foetus (gestational age), confirm a viable pregnancy and check the number of foetuses.

ANOMALY SCAN - This is done at around 20 weeks and checks for major abnormalities of the limbs or internal organs, size of the foetus, the heartbeat, the umbilical cord and the position of the placenta. Additional scans will be carried out throughout the pregnancy, if necessary, e.g. in the case of multiple births or to check foetal growth, size and wellbeing.

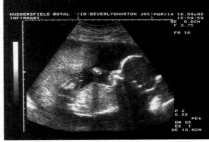

Antenatal Classes

These provide parents with an opportunity to meet other expectant parents, ask any questions they might have and learn about...
- ... the development of the unborn baby
- ... methods of pain relief in labour
- ... complications of labour
- ... relaxation techniques
- ... how to look after a new baby
- ... breast feeding

All mothers are offered screening tests in early pregnancy, but they do have the right to refuse them. The following are examples of some of the tests used:

Nuchal Fold Translucency

This can be done between 11 and 14 weeks. An ultrasound scan is used to look carefully at the fold of skin on the back of a baby's neck and to measure the amount of fluid found there. If it is thicker than normal it could indicate a baby with Down's syndrome. In most cases amniocentesis would then be offered.

Triple Test / Bart's Test (Serum Screening)

This is a blood test which may be done at 15-16 weeks. It measures the level of two hormones and a protein (AFP – alpha-fetoprotein). These three measurements are used in conjunction with the woman's age in order to estimate the possibility of her baby having Down's syndrome. A high level of AFP could also indicate an increased risk of spina bifida. Again, if there was the possibility of Down's syndrome or spina bifida, amniocentesis would be offered.

Amniocentesis

This may be done from 15 weeks onwards. A sample of the amniotic fluid, which surrounds the baby is removed using a hollow needle inserted through the abdominal wall into the uterus. An ultrasound scan has to be used to ensure that the needle is put in the correct place and no damage is done to the foetus or placenta. The amniotic fluid and the cells it contains from the foetus are examined microscopically.

The results of the test take 2 to 3 weeks and can detect...
- Down's syndrome
- spina bifida
- viral infections
- lung development
- sex

Reasons for offering amniocentesis...
- If the mother would be 37 years or older when the baby is born (i.e. older than average)
- If the mother has had a previous Down's syndrome pregnancy
- If there is a family history of chromosomal abnormality
- If any abnormality was detected by an ultrasound scan
- If a high risk was shown from a Triple, Quadruple or Nuchal Fold Test

> The detection rate in all of the above tests is about the same. If the results of any screening test indicate that there could be foetal abnormality then DIAGNOSTIC tests are used to confirm the findings.

Chorionic Villus Sampling (CVS)

This is offered at 10-11 weeks of pregnancy to women who are considered to be at high risk of having babies with Down's syndrome or inherited diseases such as sickle-cell anaemia or thalassaemia. As with amniocentesis, a hollow needle is inserted into the uterus under the guidance of an ultrasound scan. A small sample of tissue is collected from the placenta and sent to the laboratory for analysis. The results of this test take 3-4 days.

NB If problems are diagnosed from amniocentesis and CVS, some women choose to terminate their pregnancy (abortion), even though they would never have considered terminating the pregnancy previously, or they may need to prepare themselves for what lies ahead. Other women, however, refuse amniocentesis and CVS testing because they carry a risk of miscarriage or damage to the foetus.

Doppler Ultrasound

This is done in later pregnancy. It produces a 3-D image of the baby in the uterus and is used when there are complications in the pregnancy or if it is felt that the baby is not growing well. It measures the rate of the blood flow between the uterus and the baby. A consultant can use this information to ascertain, by monitoring, when the baby should be delivered.

Labour

LABOUR is the process of giving birth. It describes the period of time from the start of regular painful contractions with dilation of the cervix to the baby and placenta being delivered. Though it is not fully understood exactly how labour begins it is known to be triggered by hormonal changes.

When the mother is in labour she will, as the word implies, have to 'work hard' so that the contractions of the uterus can open the cervix and the baby can be pushed out.

> - All births are different and can take up to 24 hours from the onset of labour.
> - Though some can take place very quickly, in less than an hour, it is extremely rare.
> - First babies normally take a longer time to be born.

Labour can be divided into 3 stages:

Stage 1

During this stage the strong muscles in the uterus wall gradually open the cervix to 10cm so that it is wide enough to allow the baby's head to pass through.

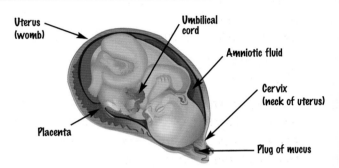

Baby in the normal position ready to be born

SIGNS OF THE FIRST STAGE OF LABOUR

SHOW
As the cervix starts to dilate (open) the plug of mucus which has sealed the neck of the uterus comes away. It may be stained with a little blood. It is not always noticed by the mother.

DIARRHOEA, BACKACHE, NAUSEA, VOMITING
These are common in the first stage of labour.

CONTRACTIONS
REGULAR and STRONG contractions start in the first stage of labour at about 20-30 minute intervals, getting stronger, more intense and closer together as labour progresses. (They should not be confused with BRAXTON HICKS CONTRACTIONS, which can be felt at any time during pregnancy and are 'practice' for labour. They are erratic, irregular and uncomfortable rather than painful. Uterus becomes tight for up to 1 minute and then relaxes again. Most common after 32 weeks).

BREAKING OF THE WATERS (RUPTURING OF THE MEMBRANES)
When the amniotic sac bursts amniotic fluid is released. The liquid (water) is clear or slightly pink. It may come out in a slow trickle or in a sudden gush.

NB Though the waters usually break in the first stage it may sometimes happen in the second stage.

Pain Relief

Pain relief is available to help the mother (see pages 34 and 35). Adopting a position which is comfortable for her personally can reduce the amount of pain and discomfort felt, e.g. lying on the side or back, propped up by pillows, supported by a bean bag, using a birthing ball, kneeling on all fours, standing, etc.

Changing position and moving around can also help, e.g. pelvic rocking. The presence of a birthing partner can also help.

Stage 2

The BIRTH CANAL is formed from the UTERUS, CERVIX and VAGINA. Very strong contractions push the baby along the birth canal. The mother will experience an overwhelming urge to 'push' and will be guided by the midwife as to when to do so in order that the head can be born gradually. When the widest part of the head emerges from the vagina it is known as 'CROWNING'. Sometimes when the head is being born a small tear can occur in the PERINEUM (the muscles supporting the contents of the pelvis). These tears can either be stitched by the midwife or left to heal naturally. Very occasionally an EPISIOTOMY may be performed (i.e. a small cut is made in the vagina) which allows the head or shoulders to pass through. This is always stitched.

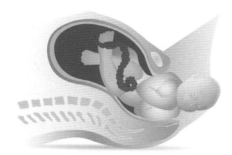

When the head emerges the baby may start to cry and breathe or it may not do so until the shoulders have been eased out. The rest of the body slides out quickly and easily and the baby is delivered onto the mother's tummy.

Once the baby is born the umbilical cord is clamped in two places. The father or midwife cuts the cord between the clamps. This is not painful and neither the mother nor the baby will feel it. The baby is now a separate person.

Stage 3

An injection of SYNTOMETRINE is given to the mother, with her consent, in order to prevent postpartum haemorrhage (excessive bleeding) and to encourage the delivery of the placenta.

The contractions will continue until the uterus expels the placenta and remaining cord. This takes 5-15 minutes. Labour is now complete.

And Finally...

Soon after birth, the baby will be fully examined (see page 39).

With the parent's permission, the baby will be given a dose of vitamin K, either shortly after birth or before they leave the delivery suite. This will be administered by mouth or by injection.

Complications During Childbirth

Childbirth is a natural physiological process, however complications can arise. For example, some babies do not lie in the head-down position. They may be in a breech, transverse or oblique position.

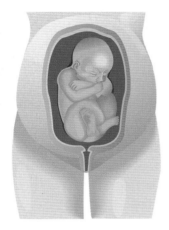

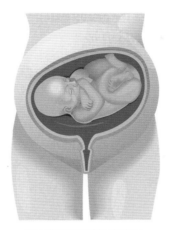

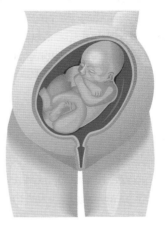

BREECH POSITION
Some babies lie in a breech position, either with their legs or bottom first. An obstetrician would assess the situation and a Caesarean section rather than a vaginal delivery might be advised.

TRANSVERSE POSITION
In this position the baby lies across the uterus and will require delivery by Caesarean section.

OBLIQUE POSITION
The baby lies at an angle in the uterus and will require delivery by Caesarean section.

NB Obstetricians sometimes attempt to manoeuvre a baby into the correct position but this is a complicated procedure, which is not always successful.

Induction

A labour will be artificially started (induced) if, for example, a baby is overdue (term +10 days) if the mother has pre-eclampsia or if the baby is failing to grow (placental insufficiency). Induction can take several days to establish labour. A combination of the following methods may be used ...

* sweeping the membranes around the baby
* artificial rupturing of the membranes using an amnihook (breaking the waters).
* prostaglandin pessary inserted into the vagina.
* intravenous drip of the hormone oxytocin (syntocinon).

Assisted Deliveries

Delivery may need to be assisted in cases of foetal distress or if the mother is unable to push the baby out herself because of exhaustion.

FORCEPS DELIVERY

Forceps (curved metal blades) are applied to either side of the baby's head and the baby is gently eased out of the vagina using the contractions. The baby is not pulled out. In most cases, this method has been superceded by the Ventouse delivery.

VENTOUSE DELIVERY

During the second stage of labour, a metal or plastic cup is attached to the baby's head by vacuum. With help from the mother and the obstetrician the baby is eased from the vagina when contractions occur.

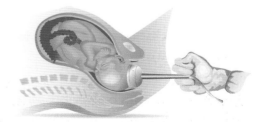

What Is A Caesarean Section?

A Caesarean section is an operation which opens up the abdominal wall and uterus in order to remove the baby. A cut is made above the pubic bone (along the bikini line) through the abdomen and uterus. The baby is removed, the cord cut and then the placenta is removed, before the uterus and abdomen are stitched. The whole procedure takes about one hour.
There are 2 types of Caesarean section...

• ELECTIVE CAESAREAN   or   • EMERGENCY CAESAREAN

Elective Caesareans

Elective Caesareans are planned ahead of time. The mother will be given a date for the operation, usually 2-3 weeks before the EDD, i.e. at 37-38 weeks of pregnancy, in the hope that the operation can be carried out before she goes into labour. When the mother goes into hospital she is prepared for the operating theatre and an epidural anaesthetic is usually administered (rather than a general anaesthetic). This means that the mother can stay awake throughout the procedure without feeling any pain and that she can hold her baby as soon as it is born.

Elective Caesareans are done for the following reasons:

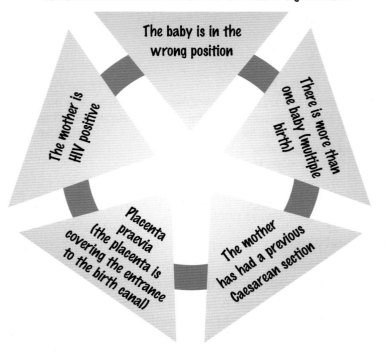

The baby is in the wrong position

There is more than one baby (multiple birth)

The mother is HIV positive

Placenta praevia (the placenta is covering the entrance to the birth canal)

The mother has had a previous Caesarean section

Emergency Caesareans

Emergency Caesareans may be performed for the following reasons:
• Foetal distress -
  if the baby is not responding well to labour it may show signs by...
    • prolonged increased/decreased heartbeat
    • passing meconium from the uterus

• These signs would be closely monitored

• Progress in labour has halted

• Severe pre-eclampsia or eclampsia in the mother

• Antepartum haemorrhaging (severe bleeding from the uterus)

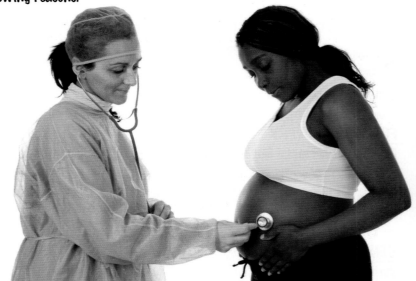

A general anaesthetic is often used during an emergency Caesarean because of the time required to set up an epidural. The mother will, therefore, be anaesthetised whilst her baby is being delivered though she will regain consciousness quite quickly.

Hand-held notes contain all the information about a woman and her baby, from her 'booking-in' visit to the post-natal examination. As the name suggests they are 'held' (kept) by the woman herself.

They will include the following information:

- Mother's name, address and a contact number
- Mother's general health and family history (general health).
- History of any previous pregnancies
- All ante-natal assessments including blood tests, screening tests, scans, blood pressure, foetal heartbeat, growth of the uterus
- Details of ante-natal admission to hospital and treatment
- Details of admission to hospital during labour
- Record of labour and delivery
- Details of any operations, e.g. stitches, Ventouse
- Examination of the neonate (new born baby)
- Post-natal observations and discharge from hospital
- Post-natal check

Advantages of hand-held notes are that they contain all the detailed information in one place, they are accessible to the woman and can prove very valuable in an emergency situation, such as premature labour in a different part of the country. A disadvantage is that they could be lost (however evidence shows that this is rarely the case). In any event, duplicate copies of scans and tests are retained by the hospital and some information is stored on computer by GPs and midwives.

Birth-plan

Women are encouraged during pregnancy to think about the experience of birth and to make plans about their ideas and expectations. These can be discussed with the midwife in detail and may be written down and kept with the hand-held notes. When in labour the birth-plan will be referred to and every effort made to accommodate the woman's wishes.
It may include the following:

- Who will be present?
- Injection of syntometrine to be given?
- Student allowed to be present?
- Female midwife preferred?
- What pain relief would be envisaged?
- Episiotomy or not?
- Baby to be given vitamin K?
- Views on monitoring during labour?
- Position for labour e.g. squatting?

Choosing The Birth Place

Women are now encouraged to choose the place in which they give birth. They are supported in their choice of HOME BIRTH or HOSPITAL BIRTH. However, there are instances in which a home birth is not advisable as hospital facilities or medical assistance may need to be provided immediately for the mother and / or baby. In such cases valuable time could also be wasted in transporting the mother and child from home to hospital.

Women will be advised against home births if...
- ... it is a multiple birth
- ... there has been a previous Caesarean section
- ... labour is premature
- ... home conditions are unsuitable
- ... there are medical problems such as high blood pressure or diabetes.

Mothers can be ADVISED about where they should give birth. If a woman chooses, AGAINST ALL MEDICAL ADVICE, to opt for a home birth rather than a hospital birth, a midwife MUST BY LAW attend to her at home. The Local Health Authority has an obligation to provide midwife cover in these circumstances.

Advantages Of A Hospital Birth

- Monitoring equipment is available to check mother and baby, e.g. cardio-tacograph
- Special equipment is available for emergency use, e.g. if Caesarean section or incubator is needed
- Midwives can share the responsibility of the baby 24 hours a day
- There are other mothers with whom to talk and share experiences
- Visiting hours restrict the number of visitors so that the mother can rest
- The mother has no domestic responsibilities such as cooking and cleaning, etc.

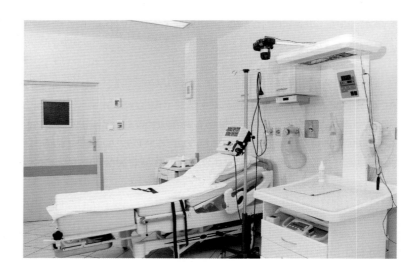

Advantages Of A Home Birth

- Familiar surroundings mean the mother is more relaxed
- The number of people present at the birth is less likely to be restricted
- The midwife will be known
- Privacy is guaranteed before, during and after birth
- The mother is not disturbed by other babies crying
- There is no routine which has to be followed, i.e. for meal times
- No transport is needed.

Home-from-home Suites

Some hospitals and maternity units have home-from-home suites which are designed to look more like hotel rooms than hospital rooms. They are intended to help make the mother feel more relaxed. They may include a kitchenette and there could be a birthing pool in the room. It would also normally have carpets, an en-suite bathroom and a double bed so that the father can stay and share the first few hours after birth with the mother. Some disadvantages are that they are sometimes in use when a mother in labour needs them; they cannot be booked in advance and they are only suitable for 'low-tech' births, for example they are not suitable if an epidural or Ventouse extraction is needed.

NOCTURNAL

At last my child sleeps,
Head laid down;
Eyes closed to the world;
Rosy cheeks quieted.

A blond square of light shines
Direct onto his pale cap,
Enlightening the calm
Beauty of a sleeping child.

Now he's safe in his own dreams,
I will rest in gentle peace

Home Births

Before the birth, the midwife will offer advice to the mother about the room in which the baby will be born. Physical comfort will be discussed, e.g. Whether the baby will be delivered on a bed, on the floor, on a bean bag, etc. Also, protective materials will be suggested for the bedding and carpet. It will be necessary to be able to control the temperature of the room and the midwife will need access to good hand washing facilities during the labour and birth.

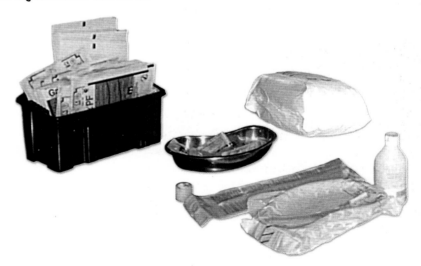

About a month before the EDD (Expected Delivery Date) the midwife will take the necessary equipment to the mother's home, e.g. cotton drapes, sterile cord clamps, scissors, etc. On attending the birth itself she will bring any necessary drugs, as well as oxygen which may be needed to resuscitate the baby.

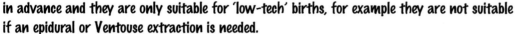

After the birth, the placenta is taken to the local maternity unit to be closely examined and disposed of safely.

Choosing The Method Of Pain Relief

Very few births are completely pain-free. However, as no two births are the same, deciding on the method(s) of pain relief before labour can be difficult.

Pregnant women have different ideas and expectations about how their pain should be managed. There are many different options and these can be discussed with the midwife at antenatal classes, parentcraft classes or clinic visits so that an informed choice can be made.

Some women do not want any interference from drugs during their labour and will consider alternative methods of pain relief; others will want to use drugs. However, it is not always possible to have the kind of pain relief envisaged and choices may alter as labour progresses.

The more relaxed the mother is the lower the level of pain is likely to be, as tension causes pain when the muscles contract.

Drugs Used For Pain Relief

Women who want to use drugs will consider...
- Entonox
- Pethidine
- Epidural Anaesthetic

EPIDURAL ANAESTHETIC
An anaesthetist inserts a hollow needle containing a fine plastic tube (catheter) into the epidural space in the lower part of the spine. The needle is removed and liquid anaesthetic administered into the tube either in a large dose which may be topped up later or by slow, continuous infusion. It stops all pain immediately by blocking the nerves in the lower body which carry messages to the brain. The mother is numb from the waist down. MOBILE EPIDURALS are the most common and allow the mother some freedom of movement during labour.

PETHIDINE
This is a drug which is injected into any deep muscle, such as the leg or bottom, to relieve pain

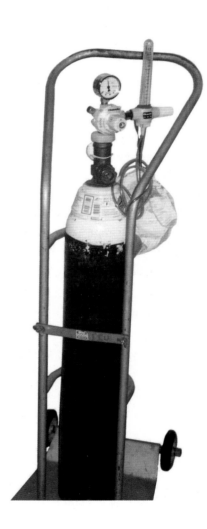

ENTONOX ('Gas & Air' or 'Gas')
This is 50% nitrous oxide (laughing gas) and 50% oxygen. It is inhaled using a mouthpiece or mask. The mother controls its use and inhalation must be started as soon as any discomfort from the contraction is felt: it takes 15 seconds to have any analgesic effect and 35 seconds to obtain maximum relief. The effects wear off in minutes. It does not harm the baby.

The Disadvantages Of Drugs

TYPE OF PAIN RELIEF	MAIN DISADVANTAGES
PETHIDINE	• The baby may be born drowsy as the drug crosses the placenta • The mother can be disorientated and feel she lacks control
ENTONOX	• Does not completely remove the pain • Mother may feel sick
EPIDURAL	• Must be administered by anaesthetist and mother must cooperate with insertion procedure • May cause headaches and backache afterwards

The Alternatives To Drugs

Women who do not want to use drugs may consider the following alternative methods:
- TENS (Transcutaneous Electrical Nerve Stimulation)
- BREATHING (Psychoprophylaxis) AND MASSAGE
- SELF-HYPNOSIS
- WATER BIRTH
- HOMEOPATHY
- AROMATHERAPY
- REFLEXOLOGY
- ACUPUNCTURE

What They Are

TENS - 4 flat pads containing electrodes are attached to the mother's back and to a monitor controlled by the mother. When she feels pain she sends electrical impulses to her back, which release endorphins in the body and blocks out pain messages going to the brain. TENS machines may be available in maternity units or can be hired from large pharmacies ahead of the EDD. No known side effects on mother or baby.

BREATHING AND MASSAGE - Relaxation exercises have to be learned at antenatal or parentcraft classes. They are especially good in the first stage of labour.

SELF-HYPNOSIS - This may be taught as an alternative method of relaxation.

AROMATHERAPY - Essential plant oils are massaged into the skin by a trained aromatherapist. The use of music furthers relaxation.

REFLEXOLOGY - Administered by a qualified reflexologist during labour and birth.

HOMEOPATHY - A trained homeopath prescribes the use of plants, herbs and minerals (with an understanding of their properties), e.g. raspberry leaves relax the uterus and arnica minimises bruising. They have no known side effects.

ACUPUNCTURE - Fine sterile needles are inserted under the skin at specific places in the body. They cause endorphins to be released which have natural anaelgesic properties.

WATER BIRTH - This takes place in a birthing pool (like a large bath), the water is kept at a constant temperature of 37°C. They encourage relaxation. They may be available in maternity units or can be hired privately for home births.

The Disadvantages Of Alternative Methods

TYPE OF PAIN RELIEF	MAIN DISADVANTAGES
TENS	• Not effective if the pain is intense • Cannot be used in a water birth and mother cannot take a bath or shower during labour
BREATHING & MASSAGE	• May not give adequate pain relief
WATER BIRTH	• Does not take all the pain away • May not be available when required
SELF-HYPNOSIS	• May not be effective. Not suitable for all women
HOMEOPATHY ACUPUNCTURE AROMATHERAPY REFLEXOLOGY	• These alternative methods of pain relief may not be enough to relieve pain • Information and training is needed from qualified practitioners before labour starts.

Special Care Baby Units (SCBU) / Neonatal Intensive Care Units (NICU)

These are units in which babies who need special medical attention are cared for. Babies sometimes need to be transferred to one of these units which have specialist cots available, however, not all maternity units have them.

Parents can visit these facilities before their baby is born. This gives them the opportunity to see all the technological equipment and to have it explained to them, thus alleviating any panic if they see their own baby in one of these units. Obviously, due to the risk of infection, this is only encouraged if it seems likely that they will need the facilities.

The units are staffed by neonatalogists and specially trained nurses and midwives. The baby may, at first, be cared for on a one-to-one basis and then, as their health improves their level of care will be reduced. Some babies only spend a few hours in a SCBU whilst others may be there for several months.

Special care baby units and neonatal intensive care units are needed by...
- some premature babies
- babies born to diabetic or drug addicted mothers
- babies who are in shock after a traumatic delivery
- babies who need immediate medical help.

Specialist Equipment

VENTILATOR
- Provides oxygen for the baby
- The oxygen is calculated and controlled to avoid brain damage
- The lungs are the last organs to mature
- An injection of a steroid is given to the mother before a premature birth to strengthen the baby's lungs (if there's time).

INCUBATOR
- The baby can be helped to breathe
- It filters and humidifies air
- It keeps the baby's temperature constant
- It keeps the baby isolated
- It's transparent so the baby can be seen clearly
- The 'Portholes' make giving attention easy

MONITOR
- This can monitor breathing, heartbeat and concentration of oxygen
- It can be linked to alarms which warn staff of any problems
- It can be linked to screens and is usually placed on baby's skin

INTRAVENOUS LINE
- This passes fluids and drugs into a baby's system
- A pump regulates the flow
- Some babies are fed intravenously if they cannot digest food

LIGHT THERAPY
- This is used to treat jaundice
- It is placed above an incubator
- Babies' eyes will need protecting from ultraviolet light

NASOGASTRIC TUBE
- Mother's expressed milk is fed directly into the stomach through a tube
- This is used if sucking / swallowing reflex has not matured
- It is also used if a baby uses too much energy in being breast or bottle fed

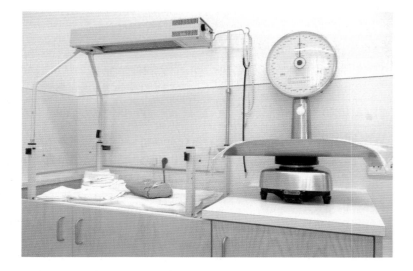

Bonding

When the feelings of love and affection grow between a parent and child it is known as bonding. This can be difficult if a baby is in SCBU. It is common for parents to feel that their baby belongs to the nurses and doctors more than themselves. Some parents may also be afraid to love a baby in SCBU in case it dies.

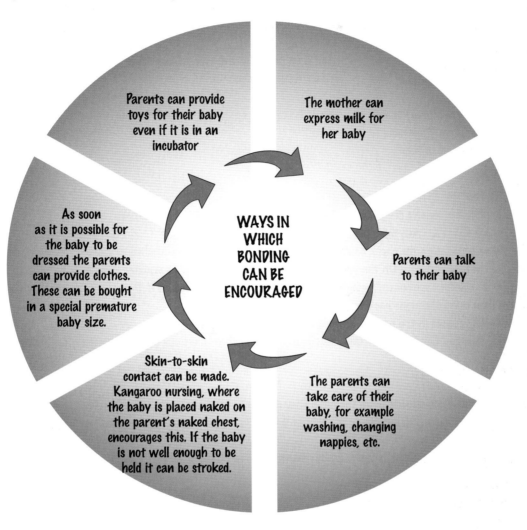

Parents can provide toys for their baby even if it is in an incubator

The mother can express milk for her baby

As soon as it is possible for the baby to be dressed the parents can provide clothes. These can be bought in a special premature baby size.

WAYS IN WHICH BONDING CAN BE ENCOURAGED

Parents can talk to their baby

Skin-to-skin contact can be made. Kangaroo nursing, where the baby is placed naked on the parent's naked chest, encourages this. If the baby is not well enough to be held it can be stroked.

The parents can take care of their baby, for example washing, changing nappies, etc.

Premature Babies

Babies which are born before their full term (i.e. before 37 weeks) are called premature babies. The earlier a baby arrives before its EDD the more likely it is to need help, especially with breathing, sucking and maintaining body temperature. Premature babies have many common characteristics. These are...

- red and wrinkled skin
- weak immune system
- inability to suck and swallow
- low calcium, iron and blood sugar levels
- inability to regulate body temperature
- underdeveloped lungs

- small size
- sealed eyes
- low birth weight
- little body fat
- yellow tint to skin (jaundice)
- large head

- 1 in 8 babies are born premature.
- Babies born at 23 weeks, weighing as little as 900g, have survived.
- More than 50% of babies born at 28 weeks survive.
- After 32 weeks the survival rate is excellent and most will survive.

Physical Characteristics

<u>FONTANELLE (SOFT SPOT)</u> - This is visible until the bones join together to form the skull at 18 months old. A tough membrane, which can be seen pulsating, protects the brain.

<u>UMBILICAL CORD</u> - This will have been clamped with a plastic clip and is visible for 7-10 days. After this time it will shrivel up and drop off.

<u>HAIR</u> - The amount and colour varies. It usually falls out and the new hair may be a different colour.

<u>EYES</u> - Babies with white skin have blue / grey eyes and those with dark skin have brown eyes. The final colour may be different and will usually be established by 12 months.

<u>SHAPE</u> - Comparatively large head, large tummy and short legs. Fat under the skin gives plumpness. When placed on the back the head will fall to one side and the arm and leg of that side stretch, whilst bending on the other side. Fists will be clenched and the soles of the feet face inwards.

<u>WEIGHT</u> - Average for full-term babies born at 40 weeks is 3.5kg. Low birth-weight babies weigh less than 2.5kg.

<u>LENGTH</u> - Average length is 50cm from head to toe.

<u>HEAD CIRCUMFERENCE</u> - Average of 35cm.

Reflex Actions

These are automatic at birth but mostly disappear by 3 months old, so they have to be 're-learnt'.

<u>SUCKING & SWALLOWING REFLEX</u> - Anything placed in the mouth will be sucked.

<u>ROOTING REFLEX</u> - When touched on the cheek babies will turn towards the side being touched, searching for the mother's nipple.

<u>WALKING REFLEX</u> - When held upright with the feet on a flat surface babies will make walking movements.

<u>FALLING REFLEX (MORO)</u> - Sudden movements which affect the neck make babies feel as if they are falling so they fling out their arms and open their hands, then bring the arms back together.

<u>GRASP REFLEX</u> - Any object placed in the hand is grasped tightly.

<u>STARTLE REFLEX</u> - Sudden bright light or loud noises cause babies to fling their arms out with elbows bent and fists clenched.

Skin

<u>MILIA</u> - Small whitish-yellow spots, especially on the nose. They disappear without treatment.

<u>VERNIX</u> - A greasy white substance which protects the skin in the uterus and after birth. It does not need to be washed off and is absorbed if left.

<u>LANGUO</u> - This is a fine layer of hair which is found mainly on the face and back; it keeps the body warm in the uterus. It is more obvious in premature babies.

Birthmarks

<u>PORTWINE STAINS</u> - May be found on any part of the body. They are permanent red / purple marks which can be camouflaged or laser treated.

<u>MONGOLIAN SPOTS</u> - This blue / grey discolouration of skin on the back or buttocks is commonly found in dark-skinned babies. It fades naturally.

<u>STRAWBERRY MARKS</u> - Bright red raised areas which appear a few days after birth and may continue to grow for several months. They start to fade and completely disappear by the time the child is 5-10 years old. Cosmetic treatment by surgery is only necessary in severe cases.

<u>STORK BITES (RED BLOTCHES)</u> - They are found on the upper eyelid, head and back of the neck. Disappear without treatment after a few years.

Senses

<u>SMELL</u> - They can recognise the smell of their mother's milk. They turn away from smells which are unpleasant.

<u>TASTE</u> - They can demonstrate a dislike for a particular taste.

<u>SIGHT</u> - Things at a distance of 20cm can be seen best. They will also react to bright lights.

<u>HEARING</u> - A new born baby is responsive to sound. They can recognise their mother's voice and other sounds they regularly heard before birth.

<u>TOUCH</u> - They can feel pain and are sensitive to skin-to-skin contact. Comfort can be provided by cuddles and being held close.

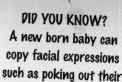

DID YOU KNOW?
A new born baby can copy facial expressions such as poking out their tongue and opening and closing their mouth.

The post-natal (puerperium) period is the time from birth to 6 weeks. The midwife and Health Visitor will be available to help and advise the mother.

The Apgar Score

At one minute after the birth and again 5 minutes later the baby (neonate) is checked using the APGAR SCORE (see below). Most babies score between 7 and 10.

	SCORES 2	SCORES 1	SCORES 0
PULSE / HEARTBEAT	100 beats per minute	Less than 100 beats per minute	No pulse
BREATHING	Regular	Irregular	None
MOVEMENTS	Active	Some	Limp
SKIN COLOUR	Pink	Bluish extremities	Totally blue
REFLEXES	Crying	Whimpering	Silent

Further checks at this stage make sure that the facial features and body proportions appear normal and that there is nothing obviously wrong with the spine, legs, fingers, toes and arms. A check on the umbilical cord looks for two arteries and one vein. The baby's temperature is checked as well as their weight, length and head circumference.

Within 24 Hours

A routine examination, with the mother present, takes place within 24 hours of the birth and is done by the paediatrician (in hospital) or midwife / GP (at home). The examination will check...

- Eyes, ears, nose
- Fontanelle
- Fingers and toes
- Abdomen
- Genitals
- Spine
- Nerves and muscles
- Chest and heart (cardio-vascular)
- Mouth (for cleft palate and teeth)
- Hip joints (for congenital dislocation)
- Arms and hands (especially for the number of creases on palm, which might indicate Down's syndrome)

NB Neonatal audiological screening tests are given to all babies to check hearing.

At 7-10 Days

A small sample of blood is taken from the baby's heel, put onto a test card and checked for...

1 <u>PKU (PHENYL-KETONURIA)</u> - also called a Guthrie test, it detects PKU. This rare condition requires a special diet if brain damage is to be prevented.

2 <u>THYROID FUNCTION</u> - if it is discovered that the hormone thyroxin is lacking, the baby can receive treatment so that its growth and development are normal and it does not have learning difficulties.

At 10 Days And 6 Weeks

Babies who are EXCLUSIVELY breastfed and were given oral vitamin K at birth will need a second and third oral dose at 10 days and 6 weeks. This is not needed by babies who are given an injection of vitamin K at birth. It is not needed by bottlefed babies.

Baby Blues And Post-Natal Depression

It is not unusual for mothers to feel miserable and down for a short period of time in the days after birth. This is due to hormonal changes, lack of sleep, fatigue after labour and the demands of a small baby. This is BABY BLUES and should not be confused with POST-NATAL DEPRESSION, which is a more long-term illness where the mother feels overwhelmed and unable to cope. Post-natal depression is treated through support from the partner and family and advice from the Health Visitor or GP. Additionally, psychiatric treatment may be given. In extreme cases it can last for several months and hospitalisation may be needed in a special mother-and-baby mental health unit. Most cases can be dealt with quickly and easily.

Post-Natal Exercises

Post-natal exercises are taught to the mother by the midwife. If practised regularly they will improve the tone of the muscles stretched during birth and delivery.

Post-Natal Examination

The post-natal examination is carried out at 6 weeks. At this time the mother has the opportunity to discuss any problems or worries regarding her baby, contraception, etc.

INTERESTING FACT!
In some cultures women are expected to remain in bed, or at least in their homes, for several weeks following the birth. In other cultures they return to their normal routine almost immediately.

POST-NATAL EXAMINATION CHECKS
- ✔ Blood pressure
- ✔ Urine
- ✔ Weight
- ✔ Routine smear test
- ✔ Emotional state of mother
- ✔ Post-natal bleeding stopped
- ✔ Size of uterus returned to normal
- ✔ Stitches used have dissolved
- ✔ Cuts and tears healed
- ✔ Baby checked to see that it's thriving

Paternity Leave

Working fathers have a legal right to take up to 2 weeks paid leave from their jobs.

After The Birth

The doctor or midwife present at the birth will notify the Local Health Authority. An NHS number is issued at this time. The birth must be REGISTERED by the parent(s) within 6 weeks so that a BIRTH CERTIFICATE can be obtained. Child benefit cannot be claimed without this. A MEDICAL CARD will also be issued so that the child can be registered with a GP.

Bottle Or Breast?

The official Government policy is to encourage all mothers to breast feed, even if only for a short period. However, women can choose to breast or bottle feed depending upon their personal circumstances. Alternatively, a combination of both can be offered by expressing milk into a bottle or supplementing breast feeds with formula milk.

Breast Feeding

All women are able to breast feed, with very few exceptions; breast size has no relevance because milk production is stimulated by birth and sucking. For the first three days COLOSTRUM is produced, which gives the baby a rich source of protein and antibodies from the mother to protect against infection. At first it is a clear, colourless liquid which later becomes yellow. When LACTATION (milk production) begins the breasts initially produce a thin, bluish milk which turns creamy at the end of a feed. The milk is squeezed out when the baby sucks the areola.

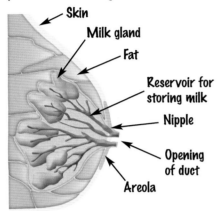

- Skin
- Milk gland
- Fat
- Reservoir for storing milk
- Nipple
- Opening of duct
- Areola

MORE SUCKING = MORE MILK PRODUCTION

By four months babies can be gradually weaned. As the feeds become fewer, or the baby refuses the breast altogether, the supply of milk will start to decrease. Some mothers, however, choose to continue breast feeding as a means of comfort for the child, perhaps at bedtime.

ADVANTAGES FOR THE MOTHER
- Bonding helped by close physical contact.
- Helps mother to regain her figure by using up kilocalories.
- If the baby is breast fed immediately after birth it helps the uterus to contract and the placenta to be expelled.
- Helps uterus return to shape after pregnancy.
- No equipment or sterilisation needed.
- It is free.
- Milk always clean and at correct temperature.
- No preparation needed and milk is always available.
- Decreases risk of breast cancer

DIFFICULTIES OF BREAST FEEDING
- Embarrassment, especially in public places.
- Concern that the baby is not getting enough milk. Overcome this by checking weight gain.
- Mother returning to work - overcome this by expressing milk and refrigerating for up to 24 hours or freezing for up to 1 month. Milk can then be given in a bottle by someone else.

ADVANTAGES FOR THE BABY
- Milk always contains the right amount of nutrients.
- Milk contains antibodies to protect from infection.
- Milk is easy to digest and never causes indigestion.
- The quality is consistent.
- Less likelihood of constipation, eczema, nappy rash, allergies, obesity and gastroenteritis in the baby.

MOTHERS WHO SHOULD NOT BREAST FEED
- Mothers who are HIV positive.
- Mothers taking recreational drugs and some prescribed drugs.
- Mothers who have had certain types of breast surgery.

DID YOU KNOW?
Wet-nursing (breast feeding for money) is one of the oldest professions. Feeding another woman's child for money has been common in all societies throughout history.

Winding

Winding (burping) can be done during or at the end of a breast or bottle feed. Babies vary in the amount of wind they get from air which they swallow. Wind causes the baby to be uncomfortable and to cry, but can be brought up quite easily by...
a) holding the baby over the shoulder and gently patting or rubbing the back or
b) sitting the baby on the knee and gently patting or rubbing the back.

Feeding Time

Bottle feeding is a perfectly good way of feeding a baby if correctly done. Special care must be taken to ensure that the baby is cuddled as much as they would have been had they been breast fed so that bonding can take place. Sit comfortably and hold the baby close giving milk at the right temperature. Make sure that the teat is kept full of milk and does not become flattened. Wind the baby if necessary.

The Equipment

BOTTLES AND TEATS are available in a wide range of shapes and sizes and choice is a matter of personal preference. It is often worth experimenting with alternatives if the baby appears to be unhappy feeding from any particular system. It is advisable to choose clear plastic bottles with a wide neck, easy-to-read measurements and a cover for the teat. The teats themselves should should allow milk to drip out freely when the bottle is held upside down. If the hole is too large it will cause the baby to choke, whilst too small a hole will cause excess wind from swallowed air.

STERILISING For the first year all feeding equipment should be sterilised to kill bacteria. This includes bottles, teats, breast pumps, bottle brushes, bowls, spoons, feeding cups, etc.

NB Sterilising in boiling water is not suitable for long-term use with plastic bottles but can be used in an emergency.

Formula Milk

Although breast milk can be given from a bottle, most bottle-fed babies are given formula milk. This is usually cow's milk (or, if this cannot be digested, soya) which has been modified to make it similar to breast milk and is usually sold in powder form. Different milks are available for different ages so that the correct nutrients are present. They have added vitamins and iron. When bottle feeding away from home a sterile bottle of boiled and cooled water can be used and a pre-measured amount of formula milk added when needed. Formula milk can be bought in pre-measured packs or it can be stored in a container designed for the purpose (this should be sterilised). If preferred the bottle can be made up before leaving home and transported in an insulated container. Pre-prepared formula milk may be more convenient when away from home as it does not need refrigerating until opened. However, it would not be advisable to use this type of formula on a regular basis as it tends to be wasteful and more expensive.

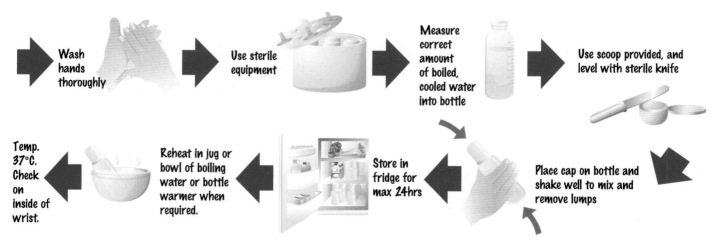

Wash hands thoroughly → Use sterile equipment → Measure correct amount of boiled, cooled water into bottle → Use scoop provided, and level with sterile knife → Place cap on bottle and shake well to mix and remove lumps → Store in fridge for max 24hrs → Reheat in jug or bowl of boiling water or bottle warmer when required. → Temp. 37°C. Check on inside of wrist.

- Bottle feeds should not be made up with more powder than stated on the packet. Too strong a feed will contain too much protein and salt and the baby will gain too much weight. More seriously, excess salt can cause convulsions, coma and permanent brain damage.
- Do not reheat milk in a microwave. 'Hot Spots' could occur and burn the baby's mouth.
- Throw away any unused milk left in a bottle. DO NOT REHEAT.
- Always check the use-by date on cartons of formula milk.
- NEVER leave babies to feed themselves, they could choke.

A Healthy Diet

Our bodies need proteins, carbohydrates, fats, vitamins and minerals for growth, repair, energy and overall good health. In a bid to improve the nation's eating habits, the Department of Health has provided some guidelines for the correct amount of nutrients needed by different groups within the community; these are called DIETARY REFERENCE VALUES (DRV).

CARBOHYDRATES
At least 5 portions a day

MEAT, FISH & PROTEIN ALTERNATIVES
2 or 3 portions a day

FRUIT & VEGETABLES
At least 5 portions a day

SUGARY & FATTY FOODS
Small amounts only of foods containing fat and sugar

DAIRY PRODUCTS
2 or 3 portions - preferably low-fat varieties

A 'healthy diet' consists of the correct DRV of nutrients for our personal needs. If the diet is varied, this is neither boring nor difficult to achieve. The Department of Health have suggested a simple model which advises on our daily intake. It is suitable for almost all people, including vegetarians, THOUGH NOT FOR CHILDREN UNDER THE AGE OF 5.

Before Conception And During Pregnancy

A healthy diet, as illustrated above, is necessary. Also, FOLIC ACID (a B vitamin) is required for 3 months before conception and for at least the first 3 months of pregnancy. This reduces the baby's chance of having spina bifida. Branflakes, white bread, broccoli, spinach, nuts and sprouts are all rich in folic acid. Alternatively, it may be taken in tablet form during this 6 month period.

Breast Feeding (Lactating) Mothers

A healthy diet aids milk production and therefore, whilst breast feeding, mothers should drink plenty of fluids and eat calcium-rich foods such as milk, cheese, canned fish, green vegetables and white bread (calcium is added by law).

Children Under 5

New research is suggesting that children's diets are now worse than ever in terms of healthy growth and development. A child under 5 needs more carbohydrates for energy and, until the age of 3, up to 15% extra fat. However, excess kilocalories will cause weight and possibly health problems, in addition to setting unhealthy eating patterns for life. Obese children are also more prone to respiratory infections. Excess weight should not be dealt with using 'reducing' or 'low-fat' diets as these are likely to fill a child up (due to high fibre content) before they have eaten enough to enable growth. The Health Visitor or GP might advise more exercise, a nutrient-dense diet or an investigation into reasons for over-eating, i.e. is the child comfort eating?

Nutrients

Parents need a good knowledge of the functions of nutrients so that they can eat healthily, set a good example to their children and provide the whole family with a balanced diet.

Macro-Nutrients

NUTRIENT	FUNCTION IN THE BODY	SOURCES
PROTEIN	GROWTH and REPAIR of cells	ANIMAL: meat, milk, fish, cheese, eggs PLANT: Beans, peas, nuts, lentils, soya, quorn, TVP, rice, cereals
FAT	To insulate the body against the COLD and to provide ENERGY	ANIMAL: meat, oily fish, butter, cream, cheese, eggs, milk PLANT: nuts, sunflower oil, olive oil, soya beans, rapeseed oil
CARBOHYDRATES SUGAR	To provide ENERGY. They also work in conjunction with protein to aid GROWTH and REPAIR	Honey, fruit, chocolate, refined sugar, e.g. granulated
STARCH		Flour, potatoes, pasta, rice, noodles, beans, cereals
FIBRE / NSP (non-starch polysaccharide)	Aids digestion. Prevents constipation	Cereals, fruit and vegetables

Micro-Nutrients

NUTRIENT	FUNCTION IN THE BODY	SOURCES
VITAMIN A	Keeps skin, eyes and mucous membranes healthy	Butter, margarine, eggs, cheese, oily fish, carrots, green vegetables
VITAMIN B COMPLEX (thiamin, niacin, folic acid, riboflavin)	Helps the release of energy from food	Bread, wholegrain cereals, milk and milk products, meat, fish, eggs, pulses, yeast and yeast extracts
VITAMIN C	Helps in the absorption of calcium and iron. Helps wounds to heal and protects against infections and allergies	Citrus fruits, strawberries, tomatoes, green vegetables, potatoes, red and green peppers
VITAMIN D	Aids absorption of calcium	Margarine and low fat spread (added by law), fatty fish, eggs. Produced under the skin by the action of sunlight (ultraviolet light).
CALCIUM	Works with phosphorus to give strength and hardness to bones and teeth	Milk, cheese, white bread (added by law), bones of canned fish, green vegetables, hard water
IRON	An important part of haemoglobin (the oxygen-carrying molecule in red blood cells). Maintains cell functions	Red meat, cocoa, plain chocolate, watercress, white bread, green vegetables, dried fruit, pulses
FLUORIDE	Helps calcium remain in bones and teeth and makes teeth resistant to the acid produced by bacteria in the mouth	Seafood and fluoridated water
IODINE	Necessary for the development of the nervous system in a foetus. Maintains body metabolism	Seafood, seaweed, milk, meat, eggs

Deficiency Diseases

If a wide variety of food is eaten over the course of a few days it is not difficult to maintain a balanced diet. If any nutrient is lacking then a DEFICIENCY DISEASE may result, though (with the exception of rickets) this is rare in Britain today. Asian babies are sometimes found to have rickets due to a lack of vitamin D, either because of their different diet, or because they are kept covered and out of sunlight or because of a combination of the two.

NUTRIENT	RESULTS OF DEFICIENCY
Protein	Kwashiorkor (severe malnutrition showing pot-bellies swollen with water)
Vitamin A	Impaired vision. Slow growth in children
Vitamin B	Beri-beri (degeneration of the nerves), pellagra (inflamed / flaky skin, diarrhoea, disorders of the nervous system), slow growth in children. Lack of folic acid can also lead to spina bifida in a developing foetus
Vitamin C	Poor skin, scurvy, slow healing wounds
Vitamin D	Rickets (bow-legs)
Calcium	Weak bones and teeth
Iron	Anaemia (reduction in the oxygen-carrying capacity of the blood)
Fluoride	Tooth decay
Iodine	Goitre (abnormally enlarged thyroid gland).

Junk Food

There are a vast range of products aimed specifically at a target market of under 5s; they are advertised and marketed as such. Even very young children will be able to identify their favourite characters on packaging. Parents need to avoid 'pester power' from their children. 'Junk food' is food which may have a high fat, salt and / or sugar content but few other nutrients, e.g. chips, crisps, cakes, biscuits, fizzy drinks / squashes and processed foods such as chicken nuggets. These fill children up and leave them unable to eat more nourishing foods. It would be unrealistic to ban them completely but they should be used in moderation or they can be adapted, e.g. baked potatoes can replace chips, beefburgers can be homemade using fresh ingredients and grilled rather than fried.

Organic Foods

These are produced without the use of chemical pesticides, fungicides or synthetic drugs. As parents have become more concerned about health, moral and ethical issues their popularity has increased. However, their nutritional content still needs to be taken into consideration.

Weaning

Weaning (mixed feeding) is the stage between the time when babies drink only milk and the time when they eat solid foods and drink other liquids. Babies usually indicate that they are ready to start being weaned by one or more of the following signs:

- Still seem to be hungry after breast or bottle feed.
- Wake up hungry in the night having previously slept right through.
- Demand food more often (go for shorter periods between feeds).

NB:
- Babies cannot cope with more salt than that found naturally in food
- Nuts should be avoided in children under 5
- Tea and coffee are not suitable for babies and young children.

Weaning can be divided into 3 stages:

Stage I (6-7 Months)

Babies are born with a supply of iron in their liver. By 6 months old this is running out and cannot be replaced by milk. They now need foods other than milk to aid their rapid growth and development. However, weaning is not advisable before 6 months unless otherwise advised by the GP or Health Visitor, as the digestive system will not be mature enough to cope and allergies in later life are more common in babies weaned early. At this age babies cannot swallow, chew or digest lumps so their food must be served at a thicker consistency (puréed), but at the same temperature as their milk.

SINGLE-GRAIN CEREALS
Rice, sago, maize, millet, cornmeal, baby rice

FRUIT
Banana, apple, peach, apricot, mango

VEGETABLES
Potato, carrot, parsnip, yam, courgette

SUITABLE FOODS AT 6 MONTHS
- The baby should be introduced to a variety of tastes and textures.
- Foods containing gluten should NOT be given. Gluten is a protein found in wheat, barley, rye and oats.
- Food can be puréed by mashing with a fork or using a sieve, blender or hand-blender.
- Fruit and vegetables should be puréed to remove any lumps.
- Excess food can be frozen in an ice cube tray for later use.
- Food may be mixed with milk, but never given from a bottle.
- To start with, food may be given from the tip of a clean finger.
- A sterilised plastic spoon should then be used.
- At first put food only on the tip as the baby must learn how to eat.

HANDY HINTS
- Start by giving a drink of milk, but not a full bottle / breast feed, before giving solid food.
- Offer solid food ONCE A DAY to begin with, IN VERY SMALL AMOUNTS. The amount of food and number of foods given can be slowly increased with time. Introduce one food at a time initially.
- Encourage with smiles and praise. Talk to the baby.
- If a food is refused DO NOT force feed, but stay calm and relaxed and try again later when it may be eaten.
- Introduce a new food by mixing it with a food you know is liked.

Stage 2 (7-9 Months)

By 6 months babies start to chew, even if they have no teeth. If no lumps are given at this stage they have difficulty learning to eat them later, therefore food should be mashed less thoroughly, or minced, so that it contains lumps which should be gradually increased in size.

SUITABLE FOODS AT 7-9 MONTHS

FRUIT
Pineapple, kiwi fruit, oranges, plums, etc.

PROTEIN
eat, fish, eggs (hard-boiled), cheese

VEGETABLES
Pulse vegetables peas, cauliflower, broccoli

- Foods containing wheat-based cereals can now be introduced
- A wider range of other foods can be introduced.
- Offer finger foods (ie. foods that they can eat with their hands)
- Give them their own spoon so that they can try to feed themselves (messy!)

> Finger foods include sandwiches, toast, low-sugar rusks, pieces of apple, banana, carrot, orange, celery, cubes of cheese, pitta bread, chapatti

- Use a beaker with two handles which they can hold (cup feeding)

Stage 3 (9-12 Months)

By now babies can be fed with the same kinds of food as the rest of the family and follow a similar feeding pattern of 3 meals a day. They will need healthy snacks and drinks in between as they only have small stomachs and use up a lot of energy, which must be replaced. At this stage they are often hungry and so are willing to try different flavours and textures. Food still needs to be mashed or chopped into small pieces if it cannot be eaten with the fingers, but they will be much more adept with a spoon by now. As the amount of solid food in the diet increases the amount of breast or bottle milk decreases until, by this stage, only a bed-time feed is needed. After 12 months a breast or bottle feed is not needed, other than for comfort. It will become increasingly difficult to give up. Milk can still be given at bedtime in a beaker or feeder cup. From 12 months onward full-fat milk may be given.

Commercially Produced Foods For Weaning

Foods which are commercially produced for weaning are available in tins, jars, bottles, packets, cartons and frozen. Their main advantage is that they are quick, easy to use and require little or no preparation – ideal for using when away from home. Dried food is useful when only a small amount of food is needed. These types of food are manufactured for different age groups. They usually have the nutritional content stated on the label. It should be remembered that they may contain additives and this will be stated on the label. During preparation, strict hygiene laws will have been adhered to, before they are packaged in tamper-proof or tamper-evident packaging so that there is no health risk involved in their use. They should not be used exclusively as they can be more expensive than the homemade equivalent and their range of taste and texture is limited.

NB Never leave children unattended whilst eating or drinking – they could choke.

Nappies

These may be disposable or re-usable. Both types are available in a wide range of shapes and sizes. Over a period of time re-usable nappies are cheaper even when the cost of laundering is taken into account. Traditional (terry-towelling) re-usable nappies have to be folded and pinned, more modern types are shaped to fit with velcro or button fastenings. Disposable nappies are convenient, absorbent, easy to use and store but are not environmentally friendly because they are not biodegradable.

Cradle Cap

This shows as greasy patches or scales, which may be red, yellow or brown in colour. It is harmless and usually clears up by itself before the child is 12 months old. It should NEVER be picked off, though it can be loosened by applying baby oil and then washing it off; alternatively special creams, designed for the purpose, may be used.

Nails

Babies' nails grow quickly and cutting them with special blunt-ended scissors prevents them scratching themselves. Nails are easier to cut after a bath when they are soft. If cooperation is a problem, wait until the baby is asleep.

Bathing

Even young babies get fluff between their fingers, grime under their nails and crusts in their eyes all of which must be removed. Bacteria from dirty nappies, urine and dribbled milk must be removed to avoid skin rashes and to keep the baby clean. Bathing not only keeps the baby clean and gives them exercise (e.g. kicking), it also allows them to relax and have close contact with an adult.

A range of moulded plastic baths are available. Baby baths can be freestanding, fit over the bath, or used on carrycot stands. Others are an unusual shape or bucket-shaped.

There are also pieces of equipment which can be used in baby baths to leave both the parent's hands free.

Topping And Tailing

This may be necessary if the baby really dislikes being bathed or if bathing is not possible.

TOP
- Use cotton wool dipped in cool, boiled water to clean the face (see step three on next page).

- Remove dribbled milk from the folds of the neck and behind the ears.

TOP
- Wipe hands and feet, unclenching the fists to clean between the fingers.

TAIL
- Remove the nappy but leave the vest on. Clean nappy area (see step two on next page).

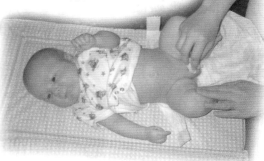

Bathing A Young Baby (Under 6 Months)

STEP ONE

- Put cold water in bath then add hot. Check temperature with thermometer or inside of wrist.
- Depth 5-8cm
- **NB** Warm room (18-21°C) with no draughts.
  It is a parental choice as to whether or not baby products are used from birth, but they are not necessary.

STEP TWO

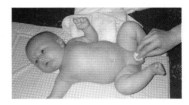

- Lie baby on changing mat or towel.
- Clean nappy area with water and cotton wool, baby lotion or nappy wipes.
- **NB** The penis and testicles of boys must be cleaned thoroughly but do NOT pull back the foreskin. Clean girls from front to back to avoid infection.

STEP THREE

- Wrap baby in soft towel (for warmth).
- Clean face with cotton wool dampened with cool boiled water.
- If necessary, clean eyes with dampened cotton wool from the bridge of the nose outwards in one movement. Throw away.
- **NB** Ears and noses are self-cleaning, DO NOT poke into them.

STEP FOUR

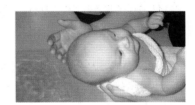

- Supporting baby's head, body and legs hold him over the bath and wash hair with a little shampoo. Rinse well.

STEP FIVE

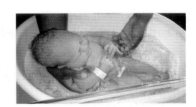

- Remove towel before lowering baby gently into the bath while supporting head, shoulders and body.
- Keep head and shoulders out of water and wash baby with cotton wool.
- **NB** Reassure the baby throughout by talking and making eye contact.

STEP SIX

- When removed from the bath, wrap the baby in a warm towel.
- Dry thoroughly by gently patting.
- Put nappy on and dress.
- **NB** If the room is warm, babies may enjoy the freedom of kicking before being dressed.

After Six Months

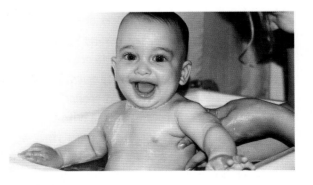

At 6 months the baby can progress to the normal family bath.
- NEVER leave the child unattended.
- Water depth 10-13cm.
- Special bath toys can be bought but empty plastic containers are just as good if not better.
- Cover hot tap with special cover or face cloth.
- Cold water added then hot. Temperature checked BEFORE child is lifted in.
- Non-slip bath mat.

Babies' Teeth

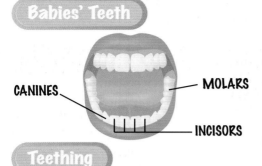

CANINES
MOLARS
INCISORS

Babies' teeth are developing before they are born. MILK TEETH (primary teeth) will begin to come through at around 6 months, with the first ones being the two central incisors on the lower jaw, followed by the central incisors of the upper jaw. The four outer incisors (two on each jaw) follow within a couple of months. All 20 are usually through by $2\frac{1}{2}$ to 3 years. After the age of 5 they begin to fall out as their roots disappear and PERMANENT TEETH replace them.

Teething

Signs of teething may be non-existent or they may be a combination of any of the following:

- sore gums
- food refusal
- dribbling
- red patch on cheek
- more cross and irritable than usual
- constantly chewing fist/hard objects

WHAT TO DO
- Comfort
- Cuddle
- Offer teething rings
- Give hard foods to chew, e.g. crusts, carrots, apple, celery, cucumber
- Distract attention

IF PAIN IS SEVERE SEEK DENTAL/MEDICAL ADVICE

Looking After Teeth

Cleaning establishes a good habit for life and avoids tooth decay, which causes pain and may make eating difficult.
The premature loss of milk teeth can cause permanent teeth to grow prematurely and in the wrong position.
PLAQUE is a soft, sticky deposit on the teeth in which many types of bacteria can flourish. These bacteria convert sugar to acid and so harm the surface of the enamel which they are in contact with. This results in some destruction of the tooth and consequently the bacteria can get inside the teeth more easily. Plaque can be removed by brushing. As soon as teeth appear they should be cleaned by the parent with a small, soft toothbrush or plastic device placed on the finger. Toothpaste especially made for children should be used in small quantities (no bigger than a pea). A wide variety of brushes, timers etc which especially appeal to children are available. As soon as children can hold a toothbrush they should be encouraged to clean their own teeth. Close supervision and help will be needed for many years to make sure that the inside of the teeth and the ones which are difficult to reach at the back of the mouth are cleaned correctly. Ideally, teeth should be cleaned after every meal, after eating sweets and definitely at bedtime. The longer the period of time that sugar is in contact with the teeth the greater the risk of tooth decay. Long before children require any dental treatment, they should be registered with a dentist. To avoid a fear of dentists, children could accompany their parents and perhaps sit in the chair to become familiar with the surroundings and equipment. A dental routine, with 6-monthly check-ups, should be established as soon as possible which will enable any treatment which is needed to take place quickly.
Hard foods such as crusty bread, carrot, apple, celery and cucumber should be encouraged as they promote healthy teeth, whilst sweet foods such as biscuits, cakes, chocolate and fizzy drinks should be limited.

(NB) Calcium, phosphorus, vitamins A, C and D all help to produce healthy teeth. Fluoride helps to prevent tooth decay. In some areas, it is added to the local water supply. If it is not added to the water, fluoride drops (under 3's) or tablets (older children) may be recommended.

Reducing Sugar In A Child's Diet

- Limit the amount of sweets, chocolate, biscuits and cakes.
- Do not add extra sugar to warm drinks.
- Do not give sweet drinks in feeding bottles as this concentrates sugar on the teeth. Feeding cups and straws are preferable. Do not allow babies to drink continuously.
- Children, especially toddlers need nutritious snacks. Try fresh / dried fruit, vegetables, plain popcorn, sugar-free breakfast cereals, unsweetened yoghurts, savoury biscuits or milk rather than sugary snack foods.
- Parents should set a good example with the foods they eat.
- Squash and fizzy drinks contain sugar (they may also be linked to hyperactivity in children). Replace them with unsweetened and diluted fresh fruit juice or better still plain water. Older children who have not been given water when younger find it harder to drink the right amount each day.

A PARASITE is an organism that lives in or on another organism and obtains its food from that organism. Chances are most children will be affected by one or more of the following parasites as they can be passed from one child to another.

PARASITE	SIGNS AND SYMPTOMS	HOW SPREAD	TREATMENT
HEADLICE	• Itchy red bite marks on scalp, especially behind ears and nape of neck • Grey / brown nits (eggs) attached to hair near scalp • White / shiny empty egg cases on hair	Head to head contact	• Leave conditioner on hair and wet-comb with detector comb to remove lice and eggs • Use chemical shampoo or treatment • Use electric comb
SCABIES	• Irritating skin rash 3 / 4 weeks after infection • Mite burrows visible • If scratched, the rash will produce septic spots on palms, between toes, fingers, armpits, groin, etc.	Direct skin-to-skin contact	• Lotion supplied by GP to treat ALL family members • Thorough washing of bedlinen, clothing and towels
FLEAS	• Small red bite marks which cause irritation especially if scratched	Jump long distances	• Ensure cleanliness of people, clothes and houses • Treat flea-ridden pets with correct treatment
THREADWORMS	• Itching around the anus, especially at night • Worms may be seen in stools or around the anus	By swallowing eggs which then hatch in the bowel	• Ensure strict hygiene, e.g. thorough handwashing, etc. • Bathe or shower each morning • Treat all the family with suitable medicine obtained from chemist or GP
ROUNDWORMS (TOXOCARA)	• Fever, vomiting, pains in muscles and joints • Eyesight can be damaged	Through animal faeces. Eggs can survive 2-4 years and may be swallowed by children	• Ensure strict hygiene precautions around pets • Dispose of animal faeces safely • Treat animals regularly for roundworms • Treat all the family with medicine from chemist or GP

NB Parasites can very easily be 'caught' but are also very easy to treat. While in general terms they cause no real harm, they are socially unacceptable!! They should be dealt with quickly before they multiply.

The Importance Of Immunisation

Babies receive antibodies via the placenta, which protect them from the same diseases as their mothers for a few months. Breastfed babies will continue to get these antibodies, with the exception of whooping cough (pertussis). After 2 months an immunisation programme is begun. The vaccines make the baby's body develop its own defence system by producing antibodies, and by the time they come into contact with other children at nursery or playgroup they are protected from infection. There are a few children for whom there is a risk of side effects from vaccinations and any worries should be discussed with the GP, especially if there have been contra-indications (a bad reaction) to a previous vaccine. Remember that a child's health is at greater risk from the diseases than from the vaccines and there are very few reasons why immunisations should not take place. However, children should not be immunised if they are unwell.

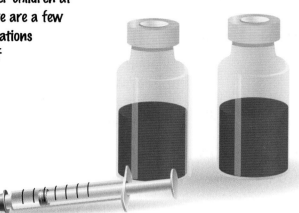

Advantages And Disadvantages Of Immunisation

ADVANTAGES
- Long-lasting protection from potentially lethal diseases
- Diseases such as polio and diptheria are now rare

DISADVANTAGES
- Red swelling at the site of the injection
- May temporarily become unwell, have mild rash or raised temperature

Immunisation Programme

AGE	VACCINE
2 MONTHS	DTaP / IPV / Hib + pneumococcal conjugate vaccine (PCV)
3 MONTHS	DTaP / IPV / Hib + MenC vaccine
4 MONTHS	DTaP / IPV / Hib + MenC + pneumococcal conjugate vaccine (PCV)
12 MONTHS	Hib / MenC
13 MONTHS	MMR + pneumococcal conjugate vaccine (PCV)

NB Each vaccine or group of vaccines represents a single injection.

Key to Vaccinations

VACCINE	PROTECTS AGAINST
d / D	Diptheria
Ta	Tetanus
P	Pertussis (Whooping Cough)
IPV	Polio
MMR	Measles, Mumps, Rubella (German Measles)
Hib	Haemophilus influenza type BC
MenC	Meningitis
PCV	Pneumoccal infection

Most childhood illnesses can be quickly and easily treated by parents. If a child is unwell then some of the following will be evident:

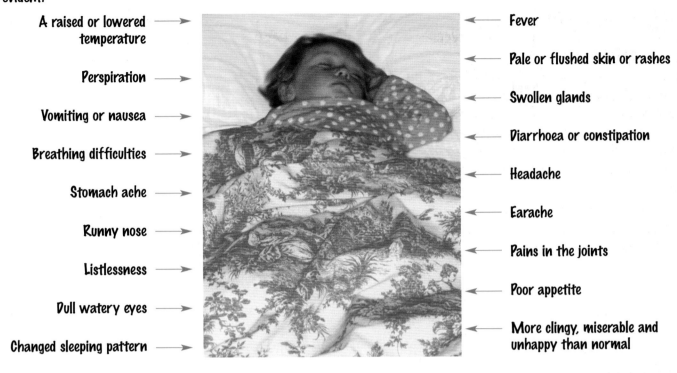

A raised or lowered temperature →

Perspiration →

Vomiting or nausea →

Breathing difficulties →

Stomach ache →

Runny nose →

Listlessness →

Dull watery eyes →

Changed sleeping pattern →

← Fever

← Pale or flushed skin or rashes

← Swollen glands

← Diarrhoea or constipation

← Headache

← Earache

← Pains in the joints

← Poor appetite

← More clingy, miserable and unhappy than normal

- These symptoms are usually caused by acquired infections (often viral) which are very common during childhood.

NB If a child is below average weight and height (failure to thrive) and is not reaching the developmental milestones for his / her age, then this may be another indication of a possible chronic health problem.

What Parents Should Do

Parents should follow their instincts if they feel their child is not well and contact a GP or Health Visitor to raise their concerns; most mothers can recognise the cry of a poorly baby. It is better to be safe than sorry!

Remember that young children do recover very quickly from childhood ailments, but immediate medical help should be sought if a child has...

- A very high temperature (over 39°C)
- A fit (convulsion)
- Breathing problems
- A purple-red rash
- Difficulty in walking or is abnormally sleepy
- Severe vomiting
- Bloody diarrhoea / stools
- Severe / persistent abdominal pain
- A stiff neck
- Swallowed a dangerous object, e.g. battery, safety pin, button, medicines, bleach, etc.

An A-Z Of Childhood Ailments

AILMENT	SYMPTOMS	TREATMENT
ASTHMA	Breathing difficulties caused by the narrowing of air passages in the lung causing 'wheezing'. Caused by infection, allergy or stress. It is also hereditary.	Use inhalers to open the airways and reduce the inflammation within the lungs.
CHICKEN POX (VARICELLA)	Small red spots which blister and scab. Mild fever, possible cough.	Calamine lotion will relieve itching. Paracetamol will reduce temperature.
COLDS	Not preventable but babies should be kept away from infected people. This is because they will have difficulty feeding if they catch a cold as they cannot breathe and suck at the same time if they have a blocked nose. Can lead to chest infections.	Use Paracetamol which is designed for babies and give plenty of fluids to drink.
COLIC	Severe abdominal pain which results in the baby crying.	Ensuring that no air is swallowed during bottle feeding and winding after a feed can help to prevent this. Use of gripe water can help. More severe wind may need prescription drugs.
CONJUNCTIVITIS (PINK EYE)	The eye is red with a yellow discharge which sticks to the eyelids.	Clean with cotton wool dipped in boiled and cooled water from the inner to the outer eye, using fresh cotton wool for each eye. Antibiotic eye drops may be needed.
CONSTIPATION	Have difficulty passing faeces.	Increase the amount of NSP (fibre) and fluids in the diet. Seek medical advice if the problem continues. Do not give laxatives.
CRADLE CAP	Can look unsightly but is harmless and nothing more than a layer of scurf (flaking skin) on the scalp.	Remove by softening first using baby oil or a commercial product and then brushing gently.
CROUP	Very harsh cough with heavy breathing and a hoarse voice.	Sudden onset requires medical attention.
DIARRHOEA	Loose watery stools are passed frequently.	Rehydration mixtures can be obtained from the chemist to replace essential salts. If it persists for more than a few hours or is accompanied by vomiting seek medical help.
EARACHE	Usually a side effect of a cold or teething.	Persistent earache requires medical attention.
ECZEMA	Scaly red rash, made worse by scratching. Found mostly on the face, behind the knees and in the creases of the elbow.	Bathing in special creams and avoiding detergents may help but it is usually outgrown by the age of 4.
IMPETIGO	Small red spots which blister and form browny-yellow crusts. Very infectious.	Can be treated quickly and effectively with antibiotics.
NAPPY RASH (AMMONIA DERMATITIS)	Skin in the nappy area becomes red and sore and septic spots may appear. Caused by ammonia being produced when urine comes into contact with bacteria in the faeces.	Remove nappy to leave skin exposed to the air. Change wet and dirty nappies frequently and apply cream after changing. If rash persists or gets worse seek medical treatment.
SCARLET FEVER	Sore throat, a bright red rash.	A course of antibiotics is needed.
TEETHING PAINS	Signs of teething are excessive dribbling, chewing on hard objects, sore gums, red cheeks and grizzling.	Relieved by comforting or distracting the baby. Provide hard food, e.g. carrot, or special hard toys to chew on.
THRUSH	Causes white patches on the tongue / in mouth. Red patches with spots if found around the genital area.	Use an anti-fungal cream or drops.
TOOTHACHE	Caused by decay. Bacteria + sugar → acid. The acid causes the teeth to decay.	Can be avoided by the correct diet, regular brushing and visits to the dentist.
TUBERCULOSIS	Coughing (phlegm contains blood), swollen glands, fever.	Very rare, so vaccine (BCG) only given to high risk groups.
VOMITING	Can be a symptom of illnesses such as gastroenteritis. Common for babies to vomit a small amount of milk after feeding (possetting). Dehydration is a possible side effect.	Possetting requires no treatment. 'Projectile' vomiting does need medical attention.

Most children will be ill at some time. The type of care they will need will depend upon their age and the length and severity of the illness. Parents can usually tell if their child is ill from the symptoms they have (see page 56) or changes in behaviour.

When Medical Help Is Required

The vast majority of childhood illnesses last from a few hours to up to a week, with the child improving steadily. They are usually treatable at home and may not need to be seen by a GP.

However, if the following symptoms are seen you should contact the GP:
- Temperature 39°C or above
- Passing no urine for 12 hours
- Abnormally fast breathing
- Severe headache
- Persistent earache
- Severe cough / difficulty breathing

These symptoms may require urgent medical help and the child should be taken to HOSPITAL:
- Convulsions (fits)
- Vomiting for more than 12 hours
- Very breathless
- A purple-red rash
- Dehydration / sunken eyes
- Sunken fontanelle (in babies)
- Severe abdominal pain for more than 12 hours
- Refusal to drink for 24 hours
- Blood in stools
- Abnormal drowsiness or floppiness

Temperature

It may be necessary to lower a high temperature to reduce the risk of febrile convulsions and to make the child feel more comfortable, especially at the beginning of an illness. This can be done by...

- Sponging or bathing the child using lukewarm water
- Removing clothing (except nappy)
- Removing bedding sheets and blanket
- Using a fan to maintain room temperature at 15°C (60°F)

A child's temperature can be checked easily. Ideally, this should be done using either an EAR or DIGITAL THERMOMETER because...
- they give accurate measurements
- their response is fast
- the figures are clear and easy to read
- they are simple to use
- they are safe to use.

FOREHEAD THERMOMETERS are made from thin plastic containing liquid crystals which change colour when held against the forehead. Forehead thermometers however, are less accurate and less easy to read. They have to be held in place carefully on the edge of the strip.

Care And Attention

Children need extra loving care when they are ill:
- Lots of comfort in the form of cuddles and extra attention ensure that they do not become bored and feel neglected.
- They need to be kept warm and comfortable, but needn't be kept in bed if they'd rather get up.
- They should be given plenty of drinks and regular paracetamol, when appropriate.
- They will need lots of different activities to keep them entertained whilst sick and convalescing (getting better but not fully recovered).
- Activities should be varied and suitable for their age; they will become bored easily. They should also be suitable to do in bed if bed-ridden, e.g. finger painting would not be suitable!
- Grandparents, siblings and friends should be encouraged to visit as soon as is appropriate; they can play and read with them, which makes entertaining easier.

A Bad Experience?

Staying in hospital can be a difficult, traumatic and upsetting experience for many children. This is because of...

- Strange surroundings
- A different bed
- A new routine
- Different food

Also, the child may be ill or in pain and may need to have treatment which is unpleasant or uncomfortable.

Making It A Happier Experience

Parents are allowed to visit at any time and stay overnight, although this is not always possible if they have other children. It is important for parents to let their child know they are missing them and when they will be visiting. If the stay is known about in advance then parents can plan for it:

- Many hospitals arrange pre-admission visits so that the child knows where they will be staying, who will be looking after them, etc. This can be reassuring; the more they understand the less worried they will be.
- The child can be shown any equipment that will be used. They can be shown what it is used for and encouraged to play with it.
- The child can pack their own bag, including their comfort toy. Perhaps they could choose something new to take with them such as pyjamas so they will look forward to staying in hospital.

As very large numbers of under 5s are admitted to hospital, it is a good idea for all parents to explain to their children about hospitals and to prepare them just in case! This can be done, depending on the age of the child, by...

- Using books, videos and telling stories

- Explaining what happens in hospital, stressing the positive aspects about being made well

- Encouraging role play by providing dressing up clothes (nurses, doctors) and 'pretend' medical equipment

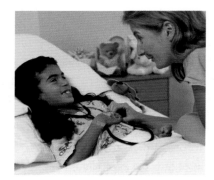

Regression

REGRESSION is when a child returns to behaviour that they showed when they were younger. It can often happen when a child is feeling insecure as they may do after a stay in hospital. Examples such as wetting the bed, temper tantrums and demanding help with feeding are common, even if they have not been problem areas for several months. Patience, understanding and lots of love and attention will solve the problem.

NB Any illness, however slight, can affect a child's developmental progress. This is usually caught up quickly when the child returns to normal health.

First Aid Box

A complete first aid box can be purchased but it is usually cheaper to put together your own. It must be easily accessible for when it is needed to treat minor accidents such as cuts, scratches, falls, scalds, burns and stings. Used items should be replaced.

NB Over-the-counter medicines such as Calpol or prescribed drugs must be kept out of the reach of children and stored and used according to the instructions given.

SUGGESTED CONTENTS OF FIRST AID BOX

- Low allergy plasters (with pictures)
- Bandages - crepe and triangular
- Gauze dressing
- Adhesive tape
- Eye bath, sterile eye pads
- Tweezers
- Calamine lotion
- Antiseptic cream
- Anti-sting cream
- Paper tissues
- Antiseptic wipes

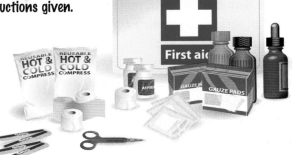

What To Do In Times Of Injury

PROBLEM	WHAT TO DO
MINOR CUTS, GRAZES AND SCRATCHES	Clean using boiled, cooled water. Pat dry gently. Leave uncovered for a scab to form unless the wound is deep enough to need a plaster.
DEEP WOUNDS	Apply pressure to stop bleeding. Seek medical help if the bleeding does not stop as stitches, butterfly stitches or a special 'glue' may be needed.
BRUISES	Apply a cold compress with firm pressure immediately after accident to prevent further bruising.
NOSE BLEED	Firmly pinch the soft part at the bridge of the nose for 10 minutes. Have the child sitting upright and slightly forward with a bowl or cloth to catch the blood if necessary. Repeat the process 3 times but if bleeding still persists seek medical help. Avoid blowing the nose for a few hours afterwards.
CHOKING	Lay a baby across the forearm with the head forwards and pat the back 4 / 5 times to dislodge the object. With an older child, put them downwards over your knee and slap 4 / 5 times between the shoulder blades. If this does not remove the object blocking the throat hold the child around their waist and get them to cough as you pull up sharply below the ribs. If this does not work, or breathing is still difficult, seek immediate medical help by dialling 999.
ELECTRIC SHOCK	If possible switch off the power, alternatively push the child away from the electrical source using a non-metallic object. Check for pulse if unconscious and resuscitate if necessary. Dial 999.
OBJECT IN THE EYE	Small objects such as dust and eyelashes, etc. can be removed from the corner of the eye using a clean cloth. When on the eyeball they should be washed away with an eye bath. Any chemicals in the eye should be washed away immediately. If the eyeball is scratched or the object is difficult to remove, seek medical help.
STINGS (FROM INSECTS AND PLANTS)	Remove an insect sting with tweezers if possible. Use calamine lotion, anti-sting or anti-histamine creams to reduce and soothe itching. For stings in the mouth get a child to suck an ice cube or ice lolly and seek medical help.
SUNBURN	Cold water, calamine or special lotions may be used to soothe the sunburn. Severe burning needs medical attention. Remember, prevention is better than cure!
BURNS (CAUSED BY DRY HEAT) SCALDS (CAUSED BY MOIST HEAT)	Small burns and scalds: Put the burnt part of the body into clean cold water for 10 minutes to remove the heat, reduce the pain and prevent scarring. Pat dry and cover with a gauze dressing if necessary. Do not use plasters, ointment, creams, butter or prick any blisters. Severe burns or scalds: Put in clean, cold water for 10 minutes. If the burn is larger than the child's hand, severely blistered or has broken skin seek hospital treatment immediately. Wrap the child in a clean COTTON sheet and get them immediately to hospital.
BROKEN BONES	With an obvious break keep the injured part immobile, stop any bleeding and seek medical help. Children's bones tend to bend as opposed to breaking, because they are still soft. Any breaks which do occur tend to be on one side only (greenstick fracture). An x-ray will determine the treatment needed.
POISONING	Telephone the doctor or take the child to the nearest hospital with a sample of the poison taken. Do not try to make the child sick.

In all situations reassure and comfort the child and stay calm.

Sleep

Neonates (newborn babies) sleep for 16–20 hours out of 24. They have individual sleep patterns but most wake about every 4 hours to be fed (smaller babies wake more often as they only have small stomachs). If they are cold, wet, uncomfortable or unwell they will wake more often. By 4 months the sleep pattern is changing and babies are awake longer during the day with 70% sleeping through the night, by 6 months most sleep through the night without needing to be fed; by 12 months babies sleep on average 12 hours at night and 2-3 hours during the day. Up to the age of 2-3 years most children continue to have an occasional nap during the day. From 3 years onwards the amount of night-time sleep begins to decrease as does the need for a day-time nap.

NB Special 'sleep clinics' are run by Health Visitors for parents who experience difficulties getting their child to sleep or who have broken nights when the child wakes them up.

Signs Of Tiredness

The classic signs of tiredness in children are...

- yawning
- dark rings under eyes
- listlessness
- wanting comforter
- sucking thumb, rubbing nose
- twiddling with hair
- not wanting to play
- crying or being more uncooperative than usual.

The Importance Of Sleep And A Regular Bedtime Routine

During periods of sleep the body produces a growth hormone; it is also a chance for the body to rest mentally and physically.

A regular bedtime routine should be established as early as possible because it helps to calm and soothe and provide security for the child. Before bedtime the level of activity should be reduced. After a warm bath and warm drink an appropriate story for the age of the child should be read or the day's activities recalled. Kisses and cuddles are important as are comfort objects or favourite toys. If the child is frightened of the dark, a special night light can be used or the bedroom door left slightly open. An attractive bedroom at a comfortable temperature will help the child to fall asleep.

NIGHTMARES
If children are over-tired or unwell they may experience nightmares. Comfort and reassurance are needed at these times.

SIDS (Sudden Infant Death Syndrome)

This is also know as 'cot death'. It usually occurs in babies between the age of 1 and 4 months. There is no warning that it will happen and, as yet, there is no proven theory as to its cause. About 500 babies each year die as a result of SIDS. It is more likely to occur in premature or low-birth weight babies and to boys. Although it is called 'cot death', it can occur in a pram, car seat or parent's arms. The following advice is given to parents and has reduced the number of deaths:

- For the first six months let the baby sleep in the same room as you.
- Lie the baby on its back in the feet-to-foot position, i.e. with the feet at the foot (bottom) of the cot.
- Do not use a pillow in the cot.
- Do not fall asleep with your baby while sitting or lying on the sofa.
- Do not share a bed with your baby if he is under 3 months old, premature, or less than 2.5kg, if you or your partner smoke, if you have been drinking alcohol, have taken medication which makes you drowsy or if you are extremely tired.
- Keep the baby in a smoke-free environment.
- Do not allow the baby to over-heat.
- Breast feed.

Fresh air, sunlight and exercise are all important qualities in a child's life if they are to remain healthy. These factors are looked at in more detail below:

Remember to
SLIP, SLAP, SLOP!
SLIP on a shirt
SLAP on a hat
SLOP on sunscreen

Do you know...
even on a cloudy
day 80-85% of the
Sun's UV rays still
reach us

Fresh Air

Being out in the fresh air is beneficial to babies and children because it improves their appetite and promotes sleep at night. An outside environment stimulates intellectual development. There is more space to play and run in the garden or park than in the house, which encourages the development of gross motor skills and muscles. Large toys such as tricycles and pedal cars can be used outdoors and it is possible to play with balls, hoops, ropes, etc. Being outside helps to promote social skills as there are more opportunities to meet a wider range of adults and children.

Sunlight

The effect of ultraviolet rays, from sunlight, on the skin produces vitamin D which aids the absorption of calcium in the body and so helps to prevent rickets. However, children should not be exposed to strong sunlight or any other extreme weather conditions. Research has shown that over exposure to the sun in childhood leads to a higher risk of cancer in adulthood. Though it is important to protect children from the elements wind, rain, snow and sun (see page 90 for information on sunscreen), it is possible to spend time outdoors most days of the year in this country as long as suitable clothing is worn so that the child does not over-heat or become very cold. Special UV protection clothing can be bought.

Exercise

Exercise in childhood improves general health, controls weight, strengthens the heart and sets a good pattern of behaviour for the future. Exercise makes children feel good and allows them to develop self-esteem and confidence in their abilities.

Safety Of Babies And Children

Parents and carers are responsible for ensuring that babies and children do not get injured. Obviously, minor mishaps will occur as children need to explore and experiment. However, a safe, hazard-free environment, with adequate supervision, should ensure that they do not come to any serious harm. Parents must be careful not to over-protect children whilst guarding them from potential danger, otherwise the child will lack confidence. All children need supervision but the amount will depend upon their age, personality and activity.

- Young babies should not be left alone on high surfaces, e.g. changing station, settee or where cats / dogs can reach them.
- By 6 months babies are mobile, mouthing (exploring objects by putting them into their mouths), and must be watched closely.
- Natural curiosity can lead to accidents as children do not see potential dangers.
- Children may try to copy others, e.g. use scissors or cut bread, but get hurt as they do not have the necessary manipulative skills.
- By 18 months to 2 years children are beginning to understand that things happen as a result of their actions, e.g. if they touch a hot radiator it will burn them.
- By the age of 3 this concept is much more refined as they learn from their experiences.
- Accidents are more likely to happen when children are excited, tired or upset as they lack concentration.

Accidents In The Home

There are many potential hazards which can cause accidents within any average home.

More than 100 under 5s die each year as a result of accidents in the home. Many more are injured, mainly due to falls.

ACCIDENT	POTENTIAL HAZARD
FALLS	Stairs / steps, windows, prams, buggies, cots, bunkbeds, carpets, rugs
CHOKING	Hard sweets, nuts, popcorn, small toy pieces
SUFFOCATION	Plastic bags, discarded fridges and freezers
CUTS	Knives, scissors, razor blades, tools
ELECTROCUTION	Sockets, any piece of electrical equipment
SCALDS & BURNS	Hot drinks, matches, lighters, fires, cookers, irons, radiators, barbecues
POISONING	Cleaning / household chemicals (methylated spirits, etc.), medications, alcohol, garden chemicals, some garden plants, berries and fungi
DROWNING	Bath, paddling pool, garden pond, bowls / buckets of water (2-3cm is enough to cause death)

Safety Symbols

The labels below show that products have been approved as being safe to use.

KITEMARK – Made to correct British Standard

BS NUMBER – British Standard (BS) number which the product conforms to.

E MARK – Comply with European Regulations.

BEAB MARK OF SAFETY – BEAB = British Electrotechnical Approvals Board. Product meets government safety regulations.

BRITISH GAS SEAL OF SERVICE – Tested and approved for safety.

TOYS

 This shows that toys have met the British Toy Manufacturers Association standards of safety.

 This shows that the European Economic Community has passed the toys as being safe.

Warning Labels

HARMFUL substances; are similar to toxic substances but less dangerous

CORROSIVE substances attack and destroy living tissues, including eyes and skin.

TOXIC substances can cause death. They may have an effect when swallowed, breathed in or absorbed through the skin.

IRRITANTS are not corrosive but can cause reddening or blistering of the skin.

Safety Precautions

Hazards can be reduced throughout the house in the following ways:

- Cover sockets
- Ensure good lighting
- Use radiator or fire guards
- Do not leave things lying around on the floor
- Safety glass / protective film, especially on internal doors
- Do not have trailing flexes
- Put springs on doors to prevent sudden closing or special strips to stop fingers being trapped

Keeping Children Safe

BATHROOM

- Wall mounted, locked medicine cupboard
- Medicines should have childproof caps
- No razors or other sharp objects accessible
- Non-slip bath (or bath mat)
- Handgrips on bath
- Shower, temperature checked for fluctuation
- Bath - cold water put in first
- Step available to reach toilet and sink
- Bathroom cleaning materials not within reach

SUPERVISE AT ALL TIMES IN THE BATHROOM

BEDROOM

- Bed away from window or radiator
- No hot water bottle in bed
- Window locks or special 'tilt and turn' windows
- No free-standing radiators
- Furniture away from window
- Bed guard (if needed)
- Cot (approved to British Standards)

KITCHEN

- Fit smoke alarm
- Use curly flexes on kettles
- Keep sharp tools in a locked drawer
- Cooker guard
- Pan handles facing inwards
- Rubbish bin emptied frequently
- High chair safe and secured with harness
- Cleaning materials locked away
- Non-slip floor
- Safety catches on washing machine, tumble dryer, fridge and freezer
- Use safety gate to keep children out OR supervise VERY closely if child is 'helping' in the kitchen
- No tablecloth on table

STAIRS & LANDING

- Safety gates at the top and bottom with childproof locks
- Stairs not slippery (if wood)
- Carpet not worn or loose
- Do not leave toys etc. on the stairs

LIVING ROOM

- No breakable ornaments within reach
- Corner guards on tables
- Video lock in operation
- Stable, solid furniture

Safety In The Garden

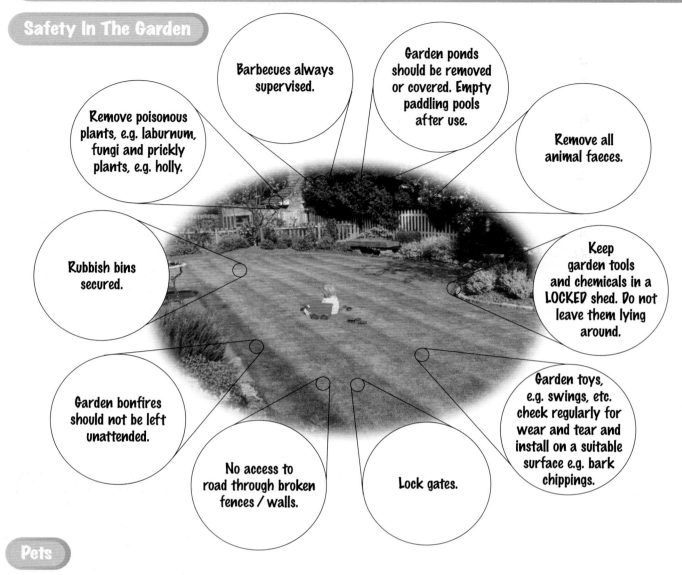

Barbecues always supervised.

Garden ponds should be removed or covered. Empty paddling pools after use.

Remove poisonous plants, e.g. laburnum, fungi and prickly plants, e.g. holly.

Remove all animal faeces.

Rubbish bins secured.

Keep garden tools and chemicals in a LOCKED shed. Do not leave them lying around.

Garden bonfires should not be left unattended.

Garden toys, e.g. swings, etc. check regularly for wear and tear and install on a suitable surface e.g. bark chippings.

No access to road through broken fences / walls.

Lock gates.

Pets

Hands should always be washed after touching pets. Pets should be checked and treated for fleas and worms regularly and should not be allowed to lick people.

Parks

In play areas of parks...
- There should be space between the equipment.
- Equipment should be in a separate fenced area.
- Slides should be set into banking or slopes.
- No glass or other rubbish on the floor.
- Swings with rubber seats.
- Special swing seats for toddlers and babies.
- Floor covering which is not hard, e.g. rubber, bark chippings.
- Different apparatus for different age groups.
- Equipment should be neither broken nor have sharp edges.

Personal Safety

Without scaring children they should be taught about 'Stranger Danger', i.e. not to go anywhere with people they do not know. If lost they are to stand still and wait until they are found and to say 'NO' if anyone makes them feel uncomfortable. Parents may use role play to get these messages across to children. They will need to be repeated often depending on the age of the child.

When Out And About

Reins or wrist straps can be useful and should be used especially near roads or in crowded places.

Supermarket Trolleys

Large supermarkets have a range of trolleys available. Always choose the correct one for the weight and age of the baby, ensuring that they are securely fastened in. Never leave the child unattended in a trolley.

Travelling by Car

It is a legal requirement for children travelling by car to be in a SAFETY RESTRAINT. Take care to always use restraints which conform to ECE Regulation 43-03. If an accident occurs whilst a child restraint system is in the car then it should be replaced as it may have been damaged. Second-hand restraints should not be used, for the same reason, unless parents can be absolutely sure of their history. All seats should be regularly checked for wear and tear.

Choosing a Safety Restraint

Always choose a child restraint for the WEIGHT and SIZE of the child not the AGE. It is a legal requirement to use the correct child resistant.

NB   Some restraints fit into more than one category shown below as they can be converted.

STAGE	GROUP	WEIGHT	AGE	OTHER INFORMATION
1	0	Up to 10kg	Birth to 6 / 9 months	Can be used in the front and back of cars.
	0+	Up to 13kg	Birth to 12 / 15 months	They often form part of a 'transport system'. Accessories such as rain covers, etc. are available.
2	1	9-8kg	9 months - 4 years	These have an integral harness and an attachment between the legs
3	2	15-25kg	4-6 years	The child is held in place with the adult seat belt. NB • The belt should be as high as possible • It should go over the pelvic region not the stomach • The diagonal strap should be on the shoulder not the neck.

If children are travelling in the front of cars, air bags must be immobilised as they can cause death or serious injury.

NB • Ensure restraints are correctly fitted into the car.
    • Adjust the straps on EVERY journey (the child may be wearing more or less clothing).
    • ALWAYS USE CHILD LOCKS ON DOORS.
    • NEVER LEAVE A CHILD UNATTENDED IN A CAR.

Areas Of Development

The four areas of development are represented by the word PIES (physical, intellectual, emotional and social). It is important to understand that these are inter-related and closely linked.

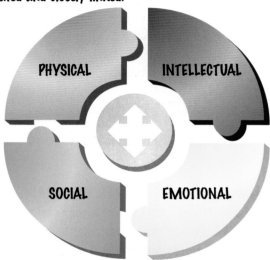

The same sequence and pattern of development can be seen in all children (except some children with disabilities). The stages which most 'normal' or 'average' children are expected to achieve by a certain chronological age are known as MILESTONES. Remember that these are only an indication because all children are different. Development can be NEGATIVELY influenced by illness, anxiety and neglect or POSITIVELY influenced by stimulation, encouragement and the opportunity to explore.

Physical Development

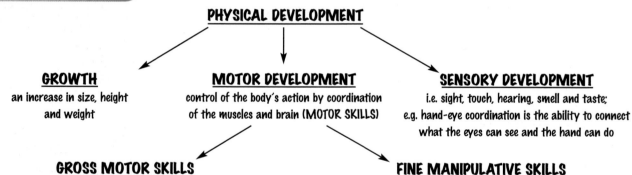

PHYSICAL DEVELOPMENT

GROWTH
an increase in size, height and weight

MOTOR DEVELOPMENT
control of the body's action by coordination of the muscles and brain (MOTOR SKILLS)

SENSORY DEVELOPMENT
i.e. sight, touch, hearing, smell and taste;
e.g. hand-eye coordination is the ability to connect what the eyes can see and the hand can do

GROSS MOTOR SKILLS
using large muscles to control the head, sitting, crawling, walking, running, jumping, hopping, squatting, climbing, etc.

FINE MANIPULATIVE SKILLS
using the hands and fingers to move, draw, fasten buttons, use a knife and fork, manipulate and carry objects, etc.

Intellectual Development

Intellectual development (cognitive and mental development) refers to a child's ability to learn, understand, recognise and reason.

Emotional Development

Young children will show a full range of emotions, from happiness to distress and from anger to fear. As they develop emotionally they will be able to recognise and control their emotions.

Social Development

It is necessary for children to develop socially so that they are able to interact and mix with others; successful social interaction leads to happier and healthier children.

Milestones In Physical Development

NEW BORN

- Walking reflex (see page 38)
- Grasp reflex (see page 38)
- When placed on front roll into a ball with head to one side
- Startled by sudden noises
- The head cannot be controlled and must be supported when lifting the baby
- Can see vague shapes, dark, light and movement
- By 1 month can 'track' objects

3 MONTHS

- When held upright legs can support a little weight
- Head still wobbles but muscles developed so there is more control
- Need support to sit up
- When on back lie with legs straight out if still. When kicking vigorously they mostly use alternate legs
- When on front can raise head and chest by supporting weight on forearms
- Hands mostly open. Can be clasped together and taken to the mouth
- Objects can be held in the hand for a few moments before being released

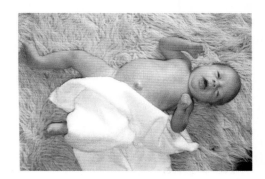

6 MONTHS

- Head fully controlled and can turn it to look around
- Can hold one or both feet when lying on back
- Can bear most of their weight when held upright and bounces up and down
- On front they can support head and chest by using straight arms
- Can sit upright using hands, buggy or pram for support
- Put objects in mouth to explore them
- Roll from back to front (front to back at 5 months)
- Hold out arms if they want to be picked up
- Point with index finger
- Reach for objects and use the whole hand (PALMAR GRASP) to pass them from one hand to another
- Turn towards their mother's voice from across a room
- Eyes work together

9 MONTHS

- Pull themselves into a sitting position and stay there for 15 minutes
- Can pull themselves into a standing position but tend to fall down rather than sit from this
- Look around to identify quiet sounds
- Crawl rapidly on hands and knees / feet, shuffle on bottom or wriggle and roll to move
- Move arms up and down together when excited
- Can walk when both hands are held
- Can use finger and thumb to grasp an object (INFERIOR PINCER GRIP)
- Can deliberately drop an object
- Look in the right place for a dropped object

12 MONTHS

- Sit unsupported for long periods
- Can rise to standing position without help from people or furniture
- Can walk with one hand held, 'cruising' along furniture, or possibly alone with feet wide apart
- Have a PRIMITIVE TRIPOD GRASP
- Can focus on objects at a distance, recognise familiar people and follow a rapidly moving object
- Can deliberately throw objects
- Help with dressing by offering an arm or foot

Milestones In Physical Development (Cont.)

15 MONTHS

- Walk alone but often fall down
- Use arms to keep balance when walking
- Walk upstairs forwards and downstairs backwards
- Can kneel
- Can use a cup and a spoon in a limited way
- Can build a tower of 2 bricks
- Help more with dressing and undressing

18 MONTHS

- Walk confidently not using arms to balance
- Walk upstairs using handrail, putting both feet on each step
- Can control wrist movements and turn doorknobs and handles
- Can use DELICATE PINCER GRASP
- Can take off shoes and socks
- Can build a tower of 3 bricks

2 YEARS

- Can run avoiding obstacles
- Use preferred hand and have good hand-eye coordination
- Can put on shoes and zip / unzip a zipper
- Can kick a ball if it is not moving
- Can move 'sit & ride' toys with feet and 'push & pull' toys with large wheels
- Can make a tower of 6 bricks
- Can see everything an adult can see
- May start to be potty trained

2 ½ YEARS

- Can walk on tiptoe and jump
- Have an improved TRIPOD GRASP
- Can thread large beads
- Use a spoon skillfully
- Can build a tower of 8 bricks
- Can pull trousers down but may have difficulty pulling them up

3 YEARS

- Walk upstairs with one foot on each stair; two on each stair to come down
- Can stand balanced on one leg and walk sideways
- Can dress and undress with some help
- Can pull trousers up and down but may need help with fastenings
- Can throw a ball overarm and catch a ball with arms extended
- Can pedal and steer a tricycle or car
- Can use scissors
- Can build a tower of 10 bricks

4 YEARS

- Can go up and down stairs with one foot on each stair like an adult
- Have MATURE PINCER GRASP
- Eat skillfully with a spoon and fork
- Improved balance: can walk along a straight line
- More skilled at ball games, using bats, etc.
- Improved skills on a tricycle
- Improved skills when dressing and undressing
- Can climb on apparatus

5 YEARS

- Can dress and undress mostly independently
- Use a knife and fork well
- Increased agility. Can skip and dance rhythmically to music
- Use large equipment confidently

An Explanation Of Intellectual Development

Intellectual development involves COGNITIVE SKILLS AND LANGUAGE SKILLS (see pages 80 and 81), i.e. it is the development of the mind and brain. It is, in general, a child's ability to learn, understand, recognise and reason. This includes imagination, creativity, reading, writing, drawing, memory, concentration, hypothesis (predicting what might happen in the future) and understanding concepts. From birth, when any of the senses are aroused, the child will attempt to make sense of what is happening. This is STIMULATION. Some people believe that children are born with their talents and abilities (intelligence) already decided by the genes they have inherited from their parents (NATURE); others believe that it is the effect of their environment (NURTURE) which is important. Much research has been done and continues about the 'Nature versus Nurture' debate. What is most likely is that intelligence is affected by both these closely interlinked factors.

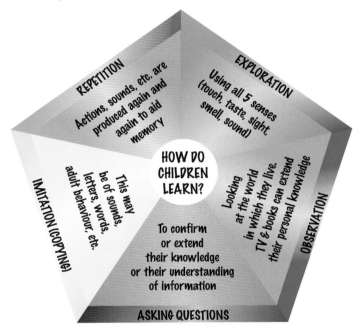

Concepts

The acquisition of concepts takes time. It starts with ideas about physical things which can be seen or felt, e.g. colours and shapes. As thinking skills become more refined they include ideas about 'abstract' things such as morals, e.g. right and wrong. Concepts include such things as...

- rhythm
- colour
- space
- light

- volume
- time
- numbers
- heat

- gravity
- size
- mass
- shape

- right & wrong
- living and non-living
- distance
- speed

Ideal Conditions For Intellectual Development

There are certain conditions which help the development of a child's intellect. Similarly other conditions may hinder a child's development. The diagram below illustrates the ideal conditions for intellectual development to take place.

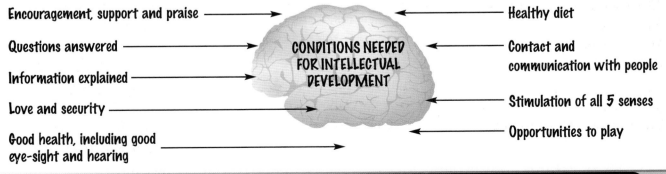

Encouragement, support and praise

Questions answered

Information explained

Love and security

Good health, including good eye-sight and hearing

CONDITIONS NEEDED FOR INTELLECTUAL DEVELOPMENT

Healthy diet

Contact and communication with people

Stimulation of all 5 senses

Opportunities to play

Toys And Games

Toys and games can be used to stimulate the intellectual development of babies and children. It must be remembered, however, that their value will be severely limited if they are simply given to the child to play with. TIME and INTERACTION with adults and other children is vital. Many activities can become more complex and be continued for years. Information about the kinds of toys which provide stimulation can be found on page 76.

Milestones

Of the four areas of development, intellectual development is the most difficult one to match to chronological 'milestones'. The information below can be used as a guideline for activities to try with a child.

NEWBORN
- Make a face for baby to copy, e.g. slide out tongue, open and close mouth.
- Hold brightly coloured, shiny or contrasting black and white patterns near to the baby and move slowly.
- Sing.
- Allow freedom to kick without clothes on (not all babies like this).

3 MONTHS
- Change baby's position (e.g. from back to front) and location (e.g. different rooms in the house, indoors and outdoors) to stimulate senses and prevent boredom.

6 MONTHS
- Action rhymes such as 'round-and-round-the-garden' and 'pat-a-cake', etc.

9 MONTHS
- 'Peek-a-boo' and 'hide and seek' type games.

12 MONTHS
- Games using hands, e.g. one potato, two potatoes etc.
- Mother and toddler groups.

18 MONTHS
- 'Feely' bag, i.e. a bag or box containing objects which the child can identify only by touch.
- Action games and songs, e.g. Wind-the-bobbin-up, The Wheels On The Bus, etc.

2-3 YEARS
- Make musical instruments and play them.
- Simple cooking and baking activities.
- Games of make believe (imaginative play).
- Visit the library, play park, etc.
- Playgroup.

Although interaction with a child is very important they also need some time on their own to solve problems and play. They should not be disrupted and given answers but allowed to find out for themselves.

3-4 YEARS
- Games such as 'sleeping logs', 'musical statues', 'musical bumps'.
- Encourage responsibility for household tasks, e.g. setting the table.
- Visit farm, zoo.

4-5 YEARS
- Visit museums, theatre, cinema.

The Emotions

Children have to learn to recognise their feelings and be able to control them. This enables them to behave in an acceptable way. Emotional development is very closely linked to social development and can also be affected by a child's state of health. Emotions can be either ☺ positive or ☹ negative...

☺ Excitement   ☺ Happiness

☺ Pleasure   ☺ Joy

☺ Pride   ☺ Contentment

☺ Affection   ☺ Love

☹ Anger

☹ Aggression   ☹ Hate

☹ Shyness   ☹ Rudeness

☹ Sadness   ☹ Guilt

☹ Frustration   ☹ Fear

☹ Jealousy   ☹ Distress

☹ Disgust

Stages Of Emotional Development

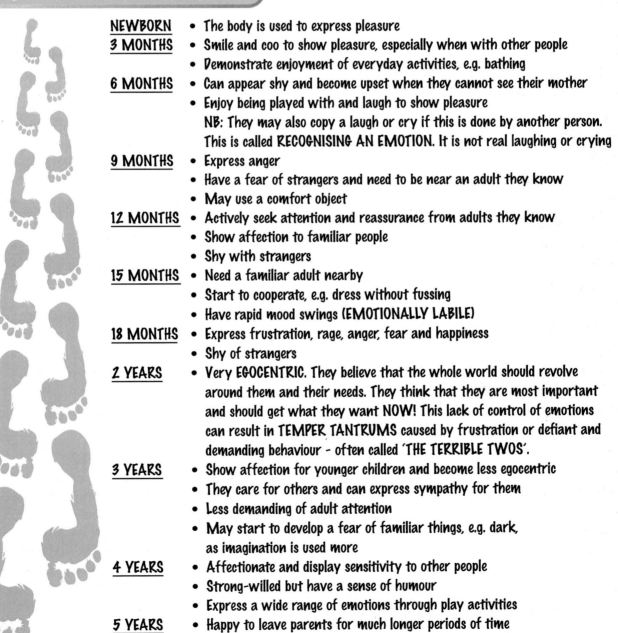

NEWBORN
- The body is used to express pleasure

3 MONTHS
- Smile and coo to show pleasure, especially when with other people
- Demonstrate enjoyment of everyday activities, e.g. bathing

6 MONTHS
- Can appear shy and become upset when they cannot see their mother
- Enjoy being played with and laugh to show pleasure
  NB: They may also copy a laugh or cry if this is done by another person. This is called RECOGNISING AN EMOTION. It is not real laughing or crying

9 MONTHS
- Express anger
- Have a fear of strangers and need to be near an adult they know
- May use a comfort object

12 MONTHS
- Actively seek attention and reassurance from adults they know
- Show affection to familiar people
- Shy with strangers

15 MONTHS
- Need a familiar adult nearby
- Start to cooperate, e.g. dress without fussing
- Have rapid mood swings (EMOTIONALLY LABILE)

18 MONTHS
- Express frustration, rage, anger, fear and happiness
- Shy of strangers

2 YEARS
- Very EGOCENTRIC. They believe that the whole world should revolve around them and their needs. They think that they are most important and should get what they want NOW! This lack of control of emotions can result in TEMPER TANTRUMS caused by frustration or defiant and demanding behaviour - often called 'THE TERRIBLE TWOS'.

3 YEARS
- Show affection for younger children and become less egocentric
- They care for others and can express sympathy for them
- Less demanding of adult attention
- May start to develop a fear of familiar things, e.g. dark, as imagination is used more

4 YEARS
- Affectionate and display sensitivity to other people
- Strong-willed but have a sense of humour
- Express a wide range of emotions through play activities

5 YEARS
- Happy to leave parents for much longer periods of time
- Enjoy caring for pets

Controlling And Expressing Feelings

It takes time for children to learn to control their feelings and they can be affected by many different circumstances. For example, bad behaviour can be the result of the death of a person or pet, boredom, frustration, tiredness, a change of routine, starting playgroup / nursery / school, a change of carer, a new baby, moving house or divorce / separation of the parents etc. Children can be encouraged to express their feelings through role play, drawing, painting, playdough, soft toys, chasing games or banging on a drum / hammering toy. Certain conditions are necessary for children to be able to develop emotionally. They need...

- ... to be reassured and helped to develop confidence and independence
- ... to bond with adults
- ... secure relationships

- ... to have high self-esteem so that self-confidence and self-reliance is possible
- ... to have socially acceptable behaviour
- ... love and affection
- ... to be valued as an individual

Negative Effects On Emotional Development

There are many things which can negatively affect the emotional development of a child as mentioned above. The following three are looked at in more detail.

SIBLING RIVALRY

Older siblings (brothers and sisters) may feel jealous when a new baby is born. They may resent the attention given to the new arrival, cling to their parents, become withdrawn, regress in behaviour, become aggressive (biting, nipping, pinching others), be uncooperative with other children or refuse to share toys.

SEPARATION ANXIETY

At 5-6 months babies think that if they cannot see something it has vanished forever; if their parents are out of sight they become worried and cry. Older children can suffer from this if they are not confident and may be upset. Give lots of love and attention, cuddles and play together. Keep separations short until the child gains confidence.

FEARS & NIGHTMARES

These often develop around the age of 2 as the imagination becomes more vivid. Sometimes they can be caused by things like moving house, starting nursery or by the separation of parents.

Developing Independence

To develop independence...
- use diversion tactics
- give control to the child over a situation wherever possible
- avoid power struggles - lead and teach rather than giving orders
- accept that defiance and disobedience are an essential part of becoming independent

- allow the child to make choices
- have reasonable expectations for the child's stage of development
- accept that it is normal behaviour for a child to do the opposite of what you want (even though this can be irritating!)

Regression

If a child feels insecure and worried their behaviour may regress (go backwards) and they will not be able to do something they have already mastered, e.g. using a potty, feeding themselves. Patience and reassurance is needed.

Bonding

This is the development of strong feelings of affection between an adult and child. The adult will be the one who has the most meaning in the child's life, and who looks after them and cares for them.

COMFORTERS

These can offer security to a child when they are faced with a new situation, separated from their parents, tired, upset or at night. A comforter may be a soft toy or a piece of blanket, sheet or clothing. The child will become very attached to it and will be extremely distressed if it is lost or misplaced. It may be needed at bedtime for several years.

Developing Social Skills

A child has to know how to act and behave in an acceptable manner so that they can fit in with the people who live with and around them. SOCIALISATION is the acquisition of a wide range of social skills such as being able to interact with other people, eat correctly, have standards of hygiene, share, take turns and understand the need for rules.

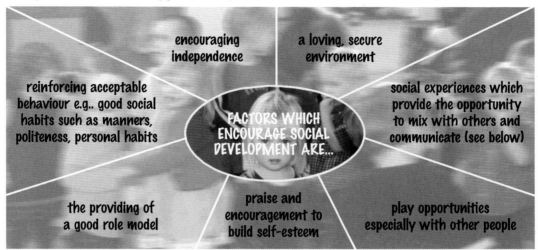

FACTORS WHICH ENCOURAGE SOCIAL DEVELOPMENT ARE...

- encouraging independence
- a loving, secure environment
- reinforcing acceptable behaviour e.g.. good social habits such as manners, politeness, personal habits
- social experiences which provide the opportunity to mix with others and communicate (see below)
- the providing of a good role model
- praise and encouragement to build self-esteem
- play opportunities especially with other people

Social Experiences

Social experiences should be appropriate to the child's age. They can include...

- ... parties
- ... holidays
- ... dance, drama or music classes
- ... shopping trips
- ... eating in a restaurant
- ... visiting a theatre, cinema
- ... visiting relatives and friends
- ... visiting a park, zoo, museum, farm
- ... nursery
- ... mother and toddler groups / playgroup
- ... ball pool
- ... swimming / gym classes

Stages Of Social Development

FIRST FEW WEEKS - Recognise sight, smell, sound and touch of main carer.
Respond with smile and gurgles.

3 MONTHS
- Have 'conversations' by making noises and enjoy the company of other people.
- Wave arms and legs and coo.

6 MONTHS
- Learn to attract the attention of adults to start interaction.
- Anxious and shy with strangers.
- Display different reactions to cross voices and pleasant voices.
- Use fingers to feed themselves.

12 MONTHS
- Can drink from a cup and use a spoon.
- Start to help with daily routines, e.g. lift legs to have nappy changed.
- Can understand and obey a simple command, e.g. 'Wave bye-bye', 'Say ta'.

2 YEARS
- Better at feeding themselves.
- Toilet training has begun.
- Try to dress themselves.
- Play near other children (parallel play).
- May not yet share toys.

3 YEARS
- Can use the toilet independently (most of the time).
- Willing to share toys and take turns in games and activities.

4-5 YEARS
- Like to be with other children, share well and understand rules.
- Can wait for adult attention, therefore less demanding.
- Can use a knife and fork, dress and undress (except for laces and buttons at the back).
- Choose their own friends.

Social Behaviour

Children must understand the difference between acceptable and unacceptable behaviour. If they don't they may regularly display NEGATIVE or ANTI-SOCIAL BEHAVIOUR which can lead to SOCIAL ISOLATION when other children do not want to play with them.

Negative or anti-social behaviour can include...
- **LYING** - if the child does not understand the difference between pretend play and real life they should be helped so that they are not confused.
- **AGGRESSION** - physical actions such as kicking, biting, punching, shouting, etc.
- **TEMPER TANTRUMS** - see page 71
- **TEASING & BULLYING** - they tease and bully other children, spoil their games and activities or damage their work / possessions.
- **SELF-HARM** - e.g. head banging.
- **ATTENTION SEEKING** - e.g. refusing to eat / use the toilet, screaming, holding their breath and refusing to cooperate with any request.

NB Attention seeking behaviour can become a habit and can be best overcome by ignoring it unless it puts the child in danger. This is not easy to do and requires a great deal of patience!

Discipline

Discipline helps children to behave in an acceptable way. It must be introduced gradually as understanding develops and must always be appropriate for a child's age and ability. Eventually children acquire self-discipline and self-control. Too much or too little parental discipline will result in a timid or badly behaved child.

Parents can show approval by...

... hugging   ... clapping
... cuddling   ... praising
... smiling   ... playing with
... touching   the child

and show disapproval by...

... not giving eye contact
... not speaking to the child
... looking disinterested
... lack of body contact (unless safety is an issue)

Good discipline requires a great deal of patience and tact and should be based on common sense.

Try not to say 'no' but if you have to make sure that it really means 'no'. Some rules are just not negotiable.

Try to look at things from a child's point of view.

Deal with any problems immediately and explain to the child what they are.

Be kind and offer praise and encouragement. Reward good behaviour. Remember, constant criticism results in poor self-image and low self-esteem.

Be firm and fair, do not expect your child to be perfect...

Do not make threats unless you know that you will carry them out.

Be reasonable and give your child a limited number of commands which you are sure they understand. Be consistent.

Parent's Guide to Discipline

WARNING!!!
Physical punishment is not effective and can be physically and psychologically damaging.

Under the age of 1, babies have no real understanding. Distraction techniques are best, or removal of the child from a situation. By 3 they should know the difference between good and bad behaviour.

Play forms a large part of every child's daily life and is one of the ways in which children learn. Playing enables them to explore and find out about their environment, practise skills, stimulates all their senses, reduce stress levels and aggression, experiment with and understand concepts, have fun and be happy. It also enables them to learn about being sad and angry.

> **There are 4 stages of play:**
>
> 1. <u>SOLITARY</u> (0-2 years) - a child plays alone, e.g. baby plays with a rattle, an older child with building bricks.
> 2. <u>PARALLEL</u> (2 years) - children play alongside but not **WITH** each other. There is no interaction.
>   Even if they are using the same toy, e.g. a toy garage, they are playing independently.
> 3. <u>LOOKING-ON PLAY</u> (3 years) - a child just watches others playing. They do not join in but may copy them.
> 4. <u>COOPERATIVE PLAY</u> (3 years +) - children play together, e.g. playing a board game, dressing-up and doing a role play, ring-a-roses, chasing games.

Types Of Play

CREATIVE

Children use their imagination and own ideas to experiment and explore with materials, music or dance. They may create something unique using playdough, paint, building bricks, card, etc. They may, on the other hand, have no end product, e.g. they may just roll and re-roll playdough to discover its properties. Creative play allows them to express their feelings and communicate their ideas which helps emotional development. If creative play is done with other children, e.g. a collage, it develops social skills. Physical development, hand-eye coordination and sensory skills are an integral part of creative play.

IMAGINATIVE (PRETEND, ROLE PLAY)

The child makes believe that they are someone else and use their imagination to become them e.g. a princess, a Teletubby. Often dressing up is involved. They may use a sheet to make a house or a row of cushions to make a car. Pretending to be another person or playing 'mums and dads' or 'schools' helps them to learn about and understand other people. Imaginative play develops confidence and allows social skills to develop if done with another child.

PHYSICAL PLAY

This is when children use their bodies in an active way so it usually requires a lot of space and may take place outdoors. Gross and fine motor skills can be developed as can coordination and balance. Examples of physical play include running, jumping, climbing, playing on a swing, slide, seesaw, riding a bike, swimming and playing football. Some of these activities can be done with other children which encourages social development and language skills. When they succeed in a physical activity their self-esteem is raised.

MANIPULATIVE PLAY

The hands, eyes and brain have to work together so it encourages physical development and intellectual development. It includes activities such as playing with a rattle or jigsaws, building with Duplo, Lego or bricks, playing with sand and water.

DISCOVERY (EXPLORATORY) PLAY

This uses all the senses, e.g. initially babies will play with their bodies and start to 'mouth' objects to find out about them by sucking or licking. Concepts such as size, shape, weight, colour and texture can be investigated and scientific and mathematical concepts learned.

SOCIAL PLAY

When children play together they learn to cooperate, take turns and share in order to make friends. They learn what is socially acceptable behaviour.

 A child may be involved in more than one type of play simultaneously.

Choosing Toys

Some toys are used over a long period of time and are replaced or upgraded as they become worn out or outgrown, e.g. a tricycle is replaced by a bike with stabilisers, Duplo bricks are used with Lego. Other toys such as rattles or playmats are used for a relatively short time. A good, successful toy should be...

- strong and stable
- safe and well-constructed
- versatile and adaptable
- suitable for the ability of the child

- suitable for the age of the child
- liked by the child and be attractive to them
- long-lasting and durable if expensive

All toys should be kept clean and checked regularly for wear and tear. Toys should always be safe to use and should have...

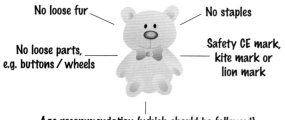

No loose fur
No staples
No loose parts, e.g. buttons / wheels
Safety CE mark, kite mark or lion mark
Age recommendation (which should be followed)

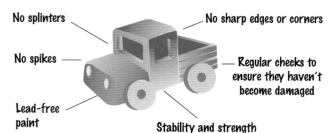

No splinters
No sharp edges or corners
No spikes
Regular checks to ensure they haven't become damaged
Lead-free paint
Stability and strength

Toys And Development

Toys help with more than one area of development, e.g. when playing with a 'ride-in-car'...

<u>SOCIAL</u> May share the car with another child by taking turns pushing them along.

<u>INTELLECTUAL</u> May be able to name parts of the car. Learn about speed and the effect of driving on different surfaces.

<u>EMOTIONAL</u> May be proud of their ability to drive the car or pleased, excited and happy about it.

<u>PHYSICAL</u> Have to use leg muscles and steering wheel to make it work which improves coordination. Have to climb in and out.

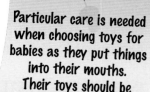

Particular care is needed when choosing toys for babies as they put things into their mouths. Their toys should be easily washable.

Toys And Age Groups

Some of the toys in the chart below may be used for much longer than the specified age, e.g. bath toys are used from 0-6 months to 5+ years.

AGE	AREA OF DEVELOPMENT	SUGGESTED TOY
0-6 mths	Sensory skills	Rattles, mobiles, soft toys, musical toys, squeaky toys, bath toys, baby mirror, suitable books (see page 66), bouncing cradle.
6-12 mths	Manipulative skills, hand-eye coordination, sensory skills, sitting and crawling	Activity mat, activity gym, stacking beakers, push and pull toys, building bricks.
12-18 mths	Hand control, speech, walking and balancing	Books, pop-up toys, sand, shape sorters, rocking toys, sit and ride toys, push and pull toys.
18mths -2yrs	Hand control, speech, walking and balancing and hand-eye coordination	Simple large-piece jigsaw, ball, Duplo, books, toys with moving parts, small swing, slide, paddling pool.
2-3yrs	Fine motor skills, gross motor skills, intellectual	Pencils, crayons, playdough, more complex jigsaw, threading beads, fuzzy-felt, picture dominoes, simple climbing frame, dressing-up clothes, books, tricycle, car, small pram, doll.
3-4yrs	Fine motor skills, gross motor skills, intellectual, pretend play, maths concepts	Bike (with stabilisers), play tent, dressing-up clothes, construction toys, simple board games, picture dominoes, materials for modelling, scissors.
4-5yrs	Precise hand-eye coordination, balance and fine motor skills, imagination	As above, plus counting games, clock, baking utensils, gardening equipment, skipping rope, rollerskates, materials for creative work.

Alternative Toys

Toys do not have to be expensive or even bought. Children can have much pleasure and enjoyment by playing with household things and objects found outdoors. Yoghurt cartons, plastic bottles, old curtains, hats, blankets, large and small empty boxes, wooden spoons, pans, washing up bowls, pinecones, twigs, leaves and shells, etc. can be utilised for a variety of play activities.

Improving Writing & Drawing

To become competent at writing and drawing, children need to have good control of the pencil, brush, etc. This is achieved by repetition and practice. They should be supplied with a range of different materials, e.g. crayons, chalk, felt-tip pens, paints and large sheets of paper in different colours, which allows them to experiment with colour, texture, shape, etc. and will prevent boredom. A 'drawing' is not always produced; sometimes a finished picture is scribbled over because the experience of using the materials is more important to the child. Often they are proud of their creation and pleased to see their work displayed. Drawing and writing allows children to express their ideas, thoughts and feelings whilst also using their imagination. As they get older they can record personal experiences.

Stages In Writing And Drawing

AGE (APPROX)	15 months	18 months	2 years	2½ years	3 years	4 years	5 years
PENCIL AND CRAYON CONTROL	PALMAR GRASP Crayon held half-way up	PRIMITIVE TRIPOD GRASP Using the thumb and first two fingers. May use preferred hand.	PRIMITIVE TRIPOD GRASP Crayon held near to the point	IMPROVED TRIPOD GRASP Uses preferred hand	DYNAMIC TRIPOD GRIP Holds pencil well and has good control.	Holds pencil well in correct way.	Good control of pencil.
DRAWING	Scribbles to and fro, not lifting crayon from paper	Scribbles to and fro but can lift crayon from paper to draw dots.	Circular squiggles. Vertical lines	Recognisable circle. Can copy / draw T and V.	Improved circle shape. Can copy H. Draws a person with squiggle features which progress to head with arms and legs.	Can copy OX. Can trace over words. Figures have head, body, legs and arms.	May write own name. Can copy △ ▢ L A C U Y
EXAMPLES							

By the age of 6 drawings have developed into much more detailed and recognisable representations. Figures have now developed from the first 'tadpole' pictures into people with more details such as eyebrows, fingers, clothes, etc. As children understand more about their environment their pictures will have sky and floor and be carefully done with details and colouring inside lines.

Books

Parents should provide a good role model by reading themselves, so encouraging children to have a positive attitude towards books. Books provide enjoyment and pleasure; they also increase vocabulary, knowledge and awareness. Children of all ages enjoy being read to and this will teach them the basics of reading (how to turn pages, follow pictures or text) and encourage intellectual development as they learn to listen and concentrate. They should have easy access to a wide range of books which avoid stereotyping and show special needs and ethnic minority people in a positive light. Books should be read during the day as well as at bedtime.

There are a wide range of books on the market, e.g. fact, fiction and poetry, etc. Many indicate the age range for which they are suitable but this is only a guideline; children know what they like and should be encouraged to choose their own books either as a 'treat' or as a present for a birthday. Local libraries have a good selection of books which can be borrowed and many also run special story-telling sessions.

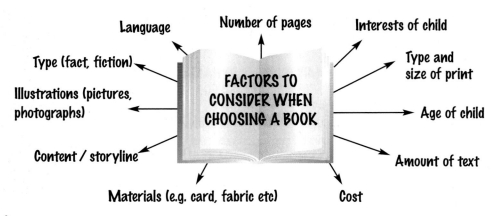

FACTORS TO CONSIDER WHEN CHOOSING A BOOK

- Language
- Number of pages
- Interests of child
- Type (fact, fiction)
- Type and size of print
- Illustrations (pictures, photographs)
- Age of child
- Content / storyline
- Amount of text
- Materials (e.g. card, fabric etc)
- Cost

NB
- Books are attractive to small babies if they show black and white shapes
- Books which clip to buggies are readily available
- Bookstart is a programme, which provides a FREE pack of books to all children at 0-12 months, 2-24 months and 3-4 years

0-1
- No words
- Up to 10 pages
- Easy to handle
- Pictures should be of familiar everyday objects, e.g. teddy, ball and they should be simple and clear.
- Should be made from strong, robust board; plastic to use in the bath; washable fabric or should contain a range of materials to 'feel'.

1-2 YEARS
- Books about their everyday activities, e.g. a visit to the park, getting dressed.
- A single line of text with clear, bold, lowercase letters.
- Simple short story (or rhymes) on a few pages.
- Sound, touch and feel activities.
- More detailed illustrations.

2-3 YEARS
- Longer, more detailed stories about imaginary characters.
- Large print.
- Lift-the-'flap or pop-up feature.
- Books which talk or make sounds when a button is pressed.

3 / 4 / 5 YEARS
- Books about normal activities / events e.g. starting school, visiting the dentist etc.
- Even longer more detailed stories with more characters.
- More text but still large print.
- Very detailed pictures.
- Humorous situations.

NB Young children often 'pretend' to read to themselves or other people. They may memorise a favourite story.

Computers

Computers and computer programmes are available for children from the age of 2, to use with supervision, and are a good tool to aid learning. They can help with number, letter and colour recognition; concepts such as size, shape and space; exploration of the wider world; using the imagination to create stories and pictures; making music.

Keyboards and mice are modified for children to make them easier to hold and control (e.g. a handball instead of a mouse).

Although computers can aid concentration and memory, they can also have a detrimental effect on the development of a child. For example, though some games can be played with others, many more are for individual children and do not encourage social interaction or language development. Other negative aspects are that they involve limited physical activity and the child may become addicted to their use and not want to do other things.

Television And Videos

There are some excellent programmes available on a wide range of TV channels and videos. These are specially produced to be suitable for children of specific ages. The benefits of television and videos are similar to those of the computer. They are most beneficial when watched WITH an adult, for a LIMITED time, and TALKED ABOUT during and after the programme. Also, they should be used as an INTRODUCTION to other activities such as imaginative play or drawing. Children should not watch adult programmes as the content is not appropriate, viewing time should be restricted and the TV should not be used as a 'babysitter'.

Crying

Communication begins at birth. Babies cry to express their needs or distress. They may be hungry, thirsty, tired, uncomfortable, in pain, bored, lonely or afraid; parents quickly learn to identify particular cries. Small babies may be left to cry for a short time but should not be left for long periods because they become hot, uncomfortable and even more distressed. If a baby continues to cry once their physical needs have been met, it may be possible to soothe them by gently stroking their body, gentle rocking, with repetitive low-pitched sounds (a voice or music) or being placed in a position where they can hear their carer's heartbeat.

Speech Acquisition

Children have to be able to control the muscles in the lips, tongue and larynx before they can make sounds. These sounds must then be coordinated in such a way that they make sense to other people. This is language. The rate at which speech is acquired varies tremendously from child to child but they all follow the same general pattern of development which is...

a) PRE-LINGUISTIC STAGE (birth to 12 months) Communication by sounds not words.

b) LINGUISTIC STAGE (12 months onwards) Single words become simple, then complex, sentences.

Lots and lots of practice is needed: PRACTICE MAKES PERFECT.

Encouraging Children To Speak

Children should be encouraged to speak by constant verbal interaction with other people from birth. When babies communicates they enjoy the attention and praise they get and this gives them the confidence to progress. Praise is important to all children and adults should never laugh at mistakes. Always give children time to speak and organise a sentence in their head if they need to do so; do not answer for them or finish sentences as this lowers their self-esteem. Speech correction should not interrupt the flow of conversation: if the child says 'I goed to the park' acknowledge what they have said by replying, 'Yes I know you went to the park' and then continue. Repeating their words in the correct form is much better than making them repeat it correctly. Encourage conversation by using 'open' questions which need more than a YES or NO answer, e.g. 'Tell me what you did at playgroup today' allows more scope than, 'Did you have a good time at playgroup today?'

> I seed my friends at playgroup

> Yes, I know you saw your friends at playgroup. What did you all do today?

Speech And Communication Therapists

These people help children who are very slow in learning to speak or who cannot speak clearly.

Stuttering (Stammering)

When children between the age of 2-4 years cannot convey their ideas quickly enough they sometimes develop a stutter. This usually passes in time and no help is needed.

IMPORTANT POINTS
- Babies and children always UNDERSTAND FAR MORE WORDS than they can speak!
- 70% of communication is NON-VERBAL (not using words).
- Non-verbal communication is...
  - facial expressions
  - intonation (the way in which things are said)
  - body language
  - eye contact

NEWBORN
- Cries.

4 WEEKS
- GUTTURAL sounds are produced from the throat.

5-6 WEEKS
- VOCALISATION – can gurgle and coo to express pleasure.

3 MONTHS
- Gurgle and babble.
- Uses vowel sounds 'aa' or 'oo'.
- Uses consonant 'ddd' or 'mmm'.
- Can take turns to speak and listen (basic art of conversation).
- Adult uses 'motherese,' i.e. a high-pitched tone of voice.

6 MONTHS
- ECHOLALIA – Can make repetitive sounds da da, ma ma, i.e. mono-syllabic babbling.
- Make sounds such as goo, der, ka, adah.

9 MONTHS
- Can make sounds such as dad-dad, mum-mum, bab-bab.
- Babbling continues.
- Try to copy sounds made by adults, e.g. coughing, blowing raspberries, smacking lips, etc.

1 YEAR
- HOLOPHRASES – an idea expressed in a single word, e.g. juice, mama, cat. These are important words to the child. (Any four-legged animal can be a 'cat', any man 'daddy').
- Sometimes use jargon, a language of their own which is only understood by those close to them.

18 MONTHS
- Use 6-40 identifiable words (more are recognisable to their carers).
- May use pivot words, e.g. teddy gone, more juice.
- Increased intonation, i.e. expression in their words.
- Echo and repeat words from from the end of adults' sentences.

2 YEARS
- TELEGRAPHIC speech where a sentence is shortened so that only the crucial words are used, e.g. daddy gone, where cat?
- These become longer, e.g. me want cake.

2½ – 3 YEARS
- Chatter constantly.
- Talk to themselves whilst playing. Verbalise actions.
- 200+ word vocabulary.
- Use pronouns 'I', 'me' and 'you' correctly.
- Can be understood by people other than family.
- Constantly ask questions – 'What's this?', 'Who's that?', 'Why?'
- Word ending sometimes incorrect, e.g. 'I runned'.

4-5 YEARS
- Talk fluently.
- Use longer, more complex sentences; basic language is understood.
- In general speech is grammatically correct.
- Most mistakes / mispronunciations have disappeared.
- Good articulation, e.g. 'yes' instead of 'yeth'.
- Jokes and riddles are enjoyed.
- Able to tell long complicated stories.
- Large ranging vocabulary (2000+ words).

Choosing The Best Option

Before choosing childcare, parents should consider the following:

Other children are being looked after.

Children are welcomed and the atmosphere in general is good.

There is a range of toys suitable for different age ranges and stages of development to encourage PIES skills.

There is a varied routine to stimulate the child.

Potential danger areas are safe.

The hours are compatible to the parents' needs.

Indoor and outdoor play.

Outings are organised.

Attitudes to potty training, sleep and discipline are acceptable.

Child seats are available if transport is used.

Staffing ratio.

Special diets can be accommodated.

Recommendations are available from other parents.

Cost.

Children are praised and encouraged.

NB Childminders should be asked about pets and smoking.

Childcare Within The Law

OFSTED
(OFFICE FOR STANDARDS IN EDUCATION)
Inspection teams look at the following areas:
EARLY LEARNING GOALS
- Personal and Social Education
- Language and Literacy
- Mathematics
- Knowledge and Understanding of the World
- Physical Development
- Creative Development

Office for
Standards
in Education

A person can only be **REGISTERED** with the local authority when their health and police records have been checked, their references verified and premises inspected for health and safety. Only after these thorough investigations have exposed no problems will they be allowed to look after children.

Full-time Childcare

Two thirds of women now return to work after having a baby, some because they do not want to take a career break, others because their income is essential. The government has recognised this situation by introducing a childcare Tax Credit Scheme which helps with the cost of childcare provision. The amount varies according to the number of hours worked, income and number of children. There is also a government web site which can help in finding local childcare: www.childcarelink.gov.uk. Full-time childcare options include: • NURSERY   • CHILDMINDER   • NANNY   • FAMILY

(NB) Emergency arrangements should always be made in case of illness.

Choosing A Full-time Option

There are advantages and disadvantages to each of the childcare options.

OPTION	ADVANTAGES	DISADVANTAGES	COST
NURSERY • For children from 6 weeks up to 5 years • Must be registered and inspected by OFSTED • May be run privately or by the state • Can attend part time	• Open from 7am to 6pm and during school holidays • Provide stimulating, safe environment • High ratio of staff to children. • Under 2's are usually in a separate area • Staff are trained and childcare is 100% reliable	• The environment is not homely • Babies may pick up more infections because there are more children to interact with	Prices vary greatly between £90–£200+ for a full week depending on the region. (Workplace nurseries may be subsidised, local nurseries are free.)
CHILDMINDER • For children from birth to 7 years • Must be registered and inspected by OFSTED • There will be an agreement to cover hours, pay, holiday, illness, overtime, etc. • Works from own home	• There is a home environment • Daily routine can be adaptable to suit individual children • Visits to parks, playgrounds, libraries, shops, etc. are more likely to take place • Flexible hours can be negotiated • May have qualifications • Siblings can be looked after together	• Care may have to be shared with several other children • Babies may pick up more infections • No back-up system if the child minder is ill	Charges vary throughout the country and are usually per hour. £75–£130+ per week, full-time
NANNY Looks after children in their own home	• Provides high quality, professional care • Child remains in an environment it is familiar with • A child's needs can be met on a personal basis • Can work very flexible hours • Sharing a nanny with another family can reduce the cost	• There could be a problem with a nanny-share agreement • Nanny may live with you or come in on a daily basis (which will cost more) • Childcare Tax Credit may not be allowable	£150–£400 per week. National Insurance and tax will also have to be paid
FAMILY Often an informal arrangement with a grandparent, aunt, sister, etc.	• Baby is in a loving home environment with a person you know well and can trust • Baby's routine and personality is known and relationships are already established	• It may be less easy to ask for the sort of care you want • It may put a strain on the relationship you have with the family member	Free or very cheap

Part-time Childcare

Some parents do not need full-time childcare, but there are still occasions when their child may be looked after by other people. This may be to give them a break or to allow the child to socialise with others.

Health Services

Family support

Education

SURESTART CHILDREN'S CENTRE

This is a place where children under 5 and their families can get help and information from a range of professionals. By 2110 the government intend to have these in every community. Surestart children's centre provides integrated...

Support with employment

Care

OUT OF SCHOOL CHILDCARE

These are open before and after school and everyday in the school holidays. They are something called 'kids' clubs'. Children can attend from the age of 3. A fee is charged.

BABYSITTERS

Babysitters look after children in their own homes for a few hours so that parents can go to places where babies and children would not be welcomed. A babysitter should be able to handle any situation which might arise and should be familiar with the child being looked after. The cost involved is usually small. In some areas special 'babysitting' courses are run for young people. Babysitters must know:

- Where the parents will be and how they can be contacted.
- The child's bedtime routine.
- Telephone number for emergency use, e.g. grandparents and GP
- Any special words the child uses e.g. for a comforter and where it is.
- Where the first aid kit is.
- Rules about TV, etc.

NURSERY SCHOOLS

These are open during school hours, term time only. Children can attend from the age of 3, starting on a morning or afternoon only basis and then attending full-time at the age of 4. They are free as part of the state education system but have to be paid for if in the private sector. From here children move on to an EARLY YEARS UNIT or RECEPTION CLASS.

PLAYGROUPS

Now called pre-schools, these are organised by trained early years professionals for children aged 2-4 years. 2 hour sessions are run in community centres, church halls, etc. at a cost of £2.50 – £5 per session. There is a staffing ratio of 1:8 and parents are expected to be involved, usually on a rota basis.

AU-PAIRS / MOTHER'S HELP

These people should never be given sole charge of babies or young children for long periods as they are not trained or experienced.

RESPITE CARE (A BREAK)

This allows parents of children with special needs to have time away from them either for a few hours, overnight or for a few days. This enables the parents to 'recharge their batteries' or spend time with other children and each other.

CRÈCHES

These are mostly run in large shopping centres. Children can be left at a small cost and are looked after by trained qualified staff whilst parents shop. Activities are organised and they are equipped with games and toys.

Special Needs

When a child's health is permanently impaired, or he / she has a learning difficulty, he / she is said to have 'special needs'. This disability may be mild or severe. It may or may not be obvious at birth and there may be one or multiple handicaps. Special needs can result from CONGENITAL DISORDERS (GENETIC PROBLEMS) which are present at birth or from OTHER EVENTS which happen during or after birth. Developmental delay is the term used when a child does not progress as expected. It affects 1-3% of the population. In about half of all children no direct cause can be found.

Congenital Disorders

DOWN'S SYNDROME

Eyes slant; eyelids have extra fold; tongue is large; head flatter at the back. Single crease across the palm.

Down's syndrome is caused by an extra chromosome. As the mother's age increases so does her risk of having a baby with Down's syndrome.

Mother's Age	Risk
25	1 in 4000
30	1 in 800
35	1 in 380
40	1 in 110
45	1 in 30

Limited intelligence makes learning a slow process.

CYSTIC FIBROSIS

This is a hereditary disease which affects the lungs. Daily physiotherapy is needed to help prevent breathing difficulties and chest infections.

It also affects the digestion and absorption of food and therefore the child does not gain weight easily.

Before birth the spinal cord is damaged, often at the lower end. Problems with mobility result. Sometimes these can be corrected by surgery. Some children can walk unaided, others have to use wheelchairs.

SPINA BIFIDA

MUSCULAR DYSTROPHY

This is a gradual weakening of the muscles which affects mobility.

CEREBRAL PALSY

If the brain is damaged by lack of oxygen at birth it can cause cerebral palsy.

Children may be affected only slightly or may have great difficulty controlling their fine manipulative and gross motor skills.

Other Events

These happen after birth and can include...
- infections such as meningitis which can injure the brain.
- accidents which can result in the loss of hearing, sight or a limb.

Nature Of Disabilities

Children may have...
a) a physical disability, e.g. blind, deaf, spina bifida, cerebral palsy.
b) an intellectual disability, e.g. autism, Down's syndrome, ADHD (attention deficit hyperactivity disorder) or
c) a combination of both.

Other Disabilities

AUTISM

This is more common in boys than in girls. Social interaction is difficult for autistic children; they have difficulty communicating with others and their use of language and speech is different.

SENSORY IMPAIRMENT

This may relate to the eyes (VISUAL) or the ears (AURAL) and can be partial or total. In both instances, the earlier the problem is detected the sooner an early intervention programme can begin. This will try to compensate for the impairment by encouraging the use of another sense, e.g. a visually impaired child would be encouraged to touch, feel and explore objects with their hands. A child with a hearing impediment will babble but make no further progress in communicating with language as they do not hear sounds around them and so cannot copy them.

Children with sensory impairments may have a STATEMENT OF EDUCATIONAL NEEDS (the child is STATEMENTED) so that they have access to the specialist teaching and equipment which they need. Wherever possible these children attend mainstream schools and nurseries. If the difficulty is severe then a specialist establishment will be needed.

Toys For Children With Disabilities

Toys should be chosen with care to match the stage of development rather than the actual age of the child. Normal toys are often suitable but a wide range should be used and changed frequently to prevent boredom and provide stimulation. Children

with visual problems benefit from brightly coloured toys which make a noise. Those with hearing problems can be given the same kind of toys and they are especially good if they move. Musical instruments allow the child to feel vibrations.

In Society

EARLY INTERVENTION PROGRAMMES

These are designed for the needs of individual children to help improve the rate of their development. They are provided with an opportunity to learn, either at home or elsewhere and are helped by a trained support worker.

OPPORTUNITY PLAYGROUPS

Aimed specifically at special needs children, they are run by specialist workers and the activities promote development. Many special needs children can attend playgroups in their own communities and may benefit from socialising with other children. Adult help may be needed.

INCLUSION POLICY

The Government's 'Inclusion Policy' aims to give all children equal rights and opportunities. Many children with special needs, who would, in the past, have attended special schools and nurseries are now integrated into mainstream schools with some support. Some special schools and nurseries remain for children with severe difficulties. After the age of 2 the child's needs are assessed by medical and educational professionals. If it is felt that these needs are 'significant and complex' the Local Authority will issue a STATEMENT OF EDUCATIONAL NEEDS. This will say what additional resources the child will need at the nursery or school, e.g. special equipment, extra support from staff. By law these resources must be provided.

Gifted Children

These children reach their 'intellectual' milestones much earlier than average. Academically they are very able. Their physical, social and emotional development will be the same as that of any other child. They may have difficulty making friends and need help to socialise with children of the same age.

Effects On The Family

Children with special needs live with their families and, like all children, should be helped to become as independent as possible. Their basic needs are exactly the same as those of any other child but, depending on the severity of their disability, extra help may be required from a range of people. Parents will have extra work in dealing with physical problems such as mobility, eating, hygiene, dressing, etc. Learning and communication problems require patience and understanding.

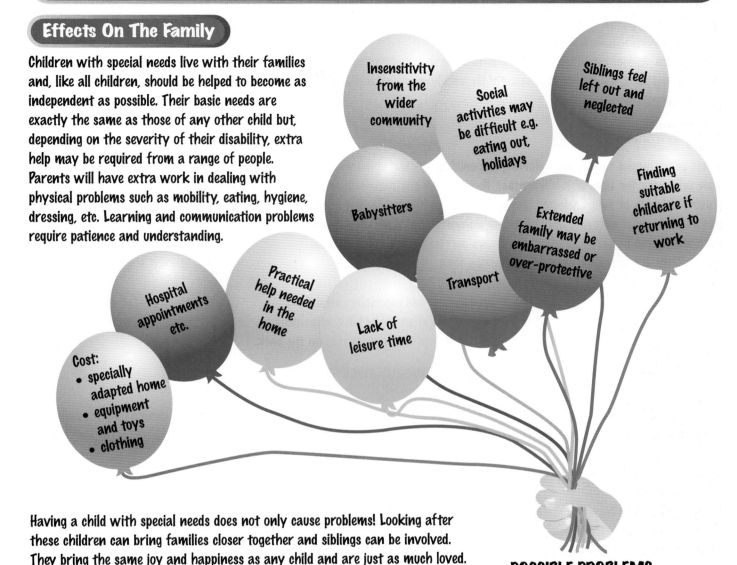

POSSIBLE PROBLEMS

Balloons:
- Insensitivity from the wider community
- Social activities may be difficult e.g. eating out, holidays
- Siblings feel left out and neglected
- Babysitters
- Finding suitable childcare if returning to work
- Extended family may be embarrassed or over-protective
- Transport
- Hospital appointments etc.
- Practical help needed in the home
- Lack of leisure time
- Cost:
  • specially adapted home
  • equipment and toys
  • clothing

Having a child with special needs does not only cause problems! Looking after these children can bring families closer together and siblings can be involved. They bring the same joy and happiness as any child and are just as much loved.

Available Help

There is help available:
- **BENEFITS** may be paid to help with care, mobility and transport.
- **LOCAL AUTHORITIES** can help with basic housing needs and adapting homes.
- **SOCIAL SERVICES** can give advice on local provisions, etc.
- **VOLUNTARY AGENCIES** can give specialist information and offer practical help and suggestions

Organisations For Special Needs

There are many organisations which help special needs children and their families. They include...
- **NDCS** - National Deaf Children's Society
- **RNIB** - Royal National Institute for the Blind
- **RNID** - Royal National Institute for the Deaf
- **SCOPE** - for people with Cerebral Palsy
- **NAS** - National Autistic Society
- **ASBAH** - Association for Spina Bifida and Hydrocephalus
- **CF FOUNDATION** - Cystic Fibrosis Foundation

Choosing Equipment

The parents' budget and lifestyle will influence the choice of equipment. It is always important for equipment to be kept hygienic and for it to be checked regularly (especially moving parts). New equipment should have the correct safety labels.

Baby Carriers

BABY SLINGS

These are strapped to the body allowing the child to be carried indoors and out, they will enjoy the close physical contact. Positions for the baby include front (facing either in or out), back and hip. They leave the hands free but should not be used whilst carrying out potentially dangerous activities, e.g. cooking. Care should also be taken to adjust the straps correctly, thus avoiding back strain. They are suitable from birth to approx. 13kg.

BACK CARRIERS

These are suitable for babies who can sit unaided and are especially useful for outdoor use. the frame is made from lightweight metal and may have attachable bags, sun canopies or rainshields. As the name suggests they are carried on the back.

Prams, Pushchairs, Buggies, Travel Systems, etc

There is a huge range of products available. Because they can be costly great care should be taken to ensure that the right choice is made. The following factors should be considered:

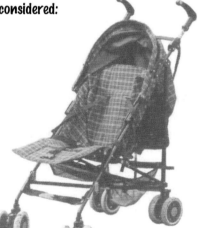

- brakes
- good suspension
- sturdiness
- storage size
- ease of adjustment
- cost
- weather resistance
- new or second hand
- accessories available
- ease of pushing and steering
- manoeuvrability
- versatility

- comfort
- ease of folding
- handle height
- weight
- tyres and wheels
- stability
- style and colour
- safety
- age range
- adjustable seat positions
- front or rear facing
- town or country use

BUGGY BOARDS

These are sturdy platforms, with or without small seats, which attach to buggies, prams and pushchairs so that toddlers can be transported.

Walking Reins

Walking reins should be used for toddlers; they assist in the control of energetic toddlers and prevent them from falling. As the child gets older reins can be replaced by a strap attached to the child's and carer's wrist (see page 65).

In The Car

CAR ACCESSORIES

These include sunshades, seat belt adjusters, booster seats, seat belt cushions, bottle and food warmers, seat back protectors and a wide range of toys.

CAR RESTRAINTS

See page 65.

Movement, Exercise And Play

BOUNCING CRADLE

These are suitable for babies up to about six months, who enjoy the movement they allow. They are easily transportable around the home and toys can be attached to them. They should only be used for short periods of time and NEVER placed anywhere other than the floor. Babies should NEVER be left in them unattended.

BABY BOUNCER

This fits in a doorway or stand and allows babies to move their arms and legs freely. They can be used from approx 4 months until the baby can walk. Babies should NEVER be left unattended.

PLAY PENS

These are available in different shapes and sizes. Because babies can see out of them they will usually play happily with toys or enjoy pulling themselves up and walking around the edge whilst parents are busy in the same room. However, some babies dislike them because their freedom is restricted. Babies do not like being left alone for more than a few minutes.

BABY EXERCISERS

These should be used with extreme care as incorrect usage causes many accidents. They do NOT help babies to walk earlier.

Feeding Time

RECLINING SEATS are available for feeding infants.

HIGHCHAIRS can be used from about 6 months when a baby can sit unaided. They should be stable, have a fitted safety harness, be easy to clean and have an adjustable tray with rounded corners. Some highchairs fold flat to save space and some can be attached to normal tables. Booster seats can be used on normal chairs where necessary.

Bedtime

COTS

These can be used from birth; babies should be placed in the 'feet-to-foot' position to prevent SIDS (see page 60). Bars should be 45-65mm apart with child-proof safety catches. Some cots have removable sides so they can be accessed from the mother's bed when the baby is small; they may convert into a small bed as the child grows. An adjustable mattress height avoids unnecessary bending. If a child can climb out of their cot they should be transferred to a normal bed where safety sides (a bed rail) can be added if necessary. Moses baskets, swinging cribs and carry cots are only useful for a few months.

TRAVEL COTS

These are useful when visiting people or for holidays. They are made from lightweight metal and fabric and fold to a compact size for easy transport. Some can also be used as a play pen.

BEDDING & MATTRESSES

Pillows should not be used. Duvets, cot quilts and baby nests should not be used under 12 months as they can lead to over-heating. Blankets are best made from cellular, acrylic material which is warm and lightweight. Sheets should be cotton, which is cool in summer and, if brushed (flannelette), warm in winter. All bedding should be washed regularly. Cot mattresses should fit snugly in the cot with no gaps where the baby could become trapped. They should be firm and, preferably, fitted waterproof sheets should be used. Some mattresses have ventilation holes at the head end. Whilst research continues into the link between SIDS and used mattresses, some experts advise that a new mattress be purchased for every new baby.

Baby Monitors

These maintain contact between the parent and child when they are not in the same place, i.e. room or garden. Some electrical or battery operated transmitters and receivers can check room temperatures and some may sound an alarm to alert the parent if the baby's breathing stops. Special TV monitors can also enable the parent to see the child.

Clothing For Babies

Babies do not need vast amounts of designer clothes! Although it is enjoyable buying and making baby clothes these will be quickly outgrown in the first few months. Babies, especially newborns, cannot control their body temperature by shivering or sweating, therefore their clothes must be suitable for the environment so they do not become too hot or too cold. Several, easy-to-remove layers are preferable. Clothes should also be easy to wash and dry.

FEATURES TO LOOK FOR WHEN BUYING BABY CLOTHES

Lightweight and loose-fitting | Flame-resistant | Easy to put on and take off | Soft and warm | Easy access for nappy changing | Non-irritant | No ribbons/open-weave fabrics - they can trap fingers

Clothing For Older Children

Clothing for older children should take into account the following factors:

- Weather conditions (hot, cold, wet)
- Bright colours
- Daywear or nightwear
- Hardwearing
- Has fastenings a child can use, e.g. velcro, large buttons, zips, poppers
- Occasion (e.g. playschool, party, seaside, etc.)
- Doesn't restrict movement
- Allows room for growth
- Allows child to use potty/toilet quickly, e.g. elasticated waist
- Is something the child likes or has chosen himself.

> **NEWBORN BABY NEEDS**
> Vests, hat, cardigans, sleepsuits, clothing for daywear, bibs, socks/bootees/mittens pramsuit, shawl (winter)

Types Of Clothes

SLEEPSUIT - Some have built-in feet which will keep the child warm in bed if they kick the covers off.
PYJAMAS - These can be bought in winter or summer thicknesses.
TROUSERS / DUNGAREES - These are especially useful when learning to crawl as knees are protected.
OUTDOOR CLOTHING - If quilted, padded or lined they will provide warmth.
HATS - They prevent heat loss from the head or provide protection from the sun.

Children In The Sun

Children should never be exposed to strong sunlight.

A suitable hat which shades the back of the neck should be worn.

Sunblock or a very high factor suntan lotion should be used (30+).

Some clothing is specially made to block out UV rays (these can cause skin cancer in later life).

Babies should be kept in the shade or under a canopy. Remember to move the pram as the sun moves position.

The feet and shoulders should be covered if the sun is hot.

Fabrics

Fabric for clothing can be NATURAL (cotton, wool, linen, silk) or SYNTHETIC (acrylic, nylon, polyester, viscose), each of which has its own properties. Generally a mixture of synthetic and natural fabrics are used to make garments more comfortable, easy to wash and hardwearing.

> If UNISEX clothing is bought it could save money by passing it on to siblings.

Children's Choice

By the age of 2 or 3 most children have very clear ideas about what they like and dislike. They should be allowed to choose their own clothes (within reason) e.g. a red or blue sweatshirt. On a daily basis they can also decide what to wear.

Babies' Footwear

'PADDERS' protect the feet when a baby is crawling. Babies do not tend to need shoes until they are walking; learning to walk barefoot makes the feet strong. Eventually, however, shoes will be needed to protect the feet from damage and to keep them warm.

> Socks, tights and the feet in sleepsuits can be outgrown, restricting the foot. These should be regularly checked for size to avoid damage.

Buying Shoes

Feet should be measured, wearing socks, regularly (at least every 3 months) as they grow rapidly up to the age of 4. Footwear can quickly become too small. If shoes are only worn for 'best' they will be outgrown before they are worn out. A wide range of styles, widths and half-sizes are available. Shoes should be fitted by trained people to ensure that they fit correctly and give good support. The bones in children's feet are soft and can be easily damaged by ill-fitting or second-hand shoes.

LIGHT

NO INSIDE SEAMS

ADJUSTABLE FASTENING

LOW HEEL

FIRM FITTING

FLEXIBLE

12-18mm GROWING ROOM AT THE TOE

SLIP RESISTANT SOLE

Types Of Footwear

SANDALS

PUMPS

WELLINGTON BOOTS

TRAINERS

These should only be worn for short periods of time as they do not meet the criteria above.

ACKNOWLEDGEMENTS

The authors and publisher would like to thank everyone who contributed to this book:

p.5   ©iStockphoto.com / Joseph C. Justice Jr.
p.7   ©iStockphoto.com / Jacob Wackerhausen
p.8   ©iStockphoto.com
p.11   ©iStockphoto.com / Joachim Angeltun
p.14   ©iStockphoto.com
p.17   ©iStockphoto.com
p.19   ©iStockphoto.com / Matjaz Boncina
p.19   ©iStockphoto.com / Heidi Kristensen
p.19   ©iStockphoto.com / Umbar Shakir
p.24   ©iStockphoto.com / Don Bayley
p.30   ©iStockphoto.com / Don Bayley
p.30   ©iStockphoto.com / Jose Manuel Gelpi Diaz
p.32   ©iStockphoto.com / Sawomir Jastrzbski
p.32   ©iStockphoto.com / Amanda Rohde
p.35   ©iStockphoto.com
p.36   ©iStockphoto.com / Dr. Heinz Linke
p.39   ©iStockphoto.com / Loic Bernard
p.42   ©iStockphoto.com / Leah-Anne Thompson
p.48   ©iStockphoto.com / Maartje van Caspel
p.49   ©iStockphoto.com / Elena Slastnova
p.51   ©iStockphoto.com / Rafik El Raheb
p.55   ©iStockphoto.com / Monika Adamczyk
p.58   ©iStockphoto.com / Steve Cole
p.58   ©iStockphoto.com
p.60   ©iStockphoto.com / Diane Diederich
p.85   ©iStockphoto.com / Kenneth C. Zirkel

Every effort has been made to contact the holders of copyright material, but if any have been inadvertently overlooked, the Publishers will be pleased to make the necessary arrangements at the first opportunity.

ISBN 978-1-905896-05-9

Published by Letts and Lonsdale.

Letts and Lonsdale make every effort to ensure that all paper used in our books is made from wood pulp obtained from sustainable and well-managed forests.